호텔관광 실무영어

English for Hospitality & Tourism Industry

In the hotel and tourism industries English language skills are both a daily requirement and essential for career advancement

Choi, Yong Son
Wang, Young Gyun

정문각

PREFACE

The hospitality industry is one that is primarily focused on customer satisfaction. The hospitality industry covers a wide range of organizations offering food service and accommodation. For the most part, it is built on leisure or is luxury-based, as opposed to meeting basic needs. Hotels and resorts, restaurants, cruise lines, event planning, theme parks, transportation, airlines and other various forms of tourism all generally fall under the realm of the hospitality industry.

Do you work in the hotel industry? Do you teach English to people in the hotel industry? If so, then this book may be just for you. This book provides basic English training for employees of the hotel industry who wish to improve their English skills. The lessons are function based and contain common hotel English expressions for the various functions that are likely to be encountered by hotel employees. Sample dialogues are also included that students may use as models.

The sole hope of this book is to improve the English used in hotels by hotel employees. Improving English skills by hotel staff can result in improved services to hotel guests, enhance the person's employ ability, and just maybe increase their income stream by increasing the size of their tips.

English has become the universal language for the hospitality industry. Whether you work in a hotel in Dubai, a restaurant in Paris, or a casino in Bangkok, chances are that you will have to speak English to some of your customers.

In the hotel and tourism industries English language skills are both a daily requirement and essential for career advancement. English for Hospitality & Tourism Industry is specifically designed for young adults wishing to enter the international hotel and hospitality field for the purpose of improving their English.

Table of Contents

Chapter

01 Reservation

Conversation : I want to make a reservation.

(Over the Phone)

Receptionist : Good afternoon, This is Marriott Hotel. How can I help you?

Mr. Green : I'd like to make a reservation for a room.

Receptionist : Could I have your name, please?

Mr. Green : Oh yes, Mr. Green.

Receptionist : What type of room do you want?

Mr. Green : I'd like a room with a double bed.

Receptionist: How long will you be staying with us, Mr. Green?

Mr. Green : From Sunday December the 1st until Thursday December the 5th.

Receptionist : All right. I'll need your contact number and credit card details as a deposit, please.

Mr. Green : OK, my phone number is 010-8356-2643 and my VISA number is 4312 5643 7856 9876.

Receptionist : Your reservation has been made. We look forward to seeing you on Sunday December 1st.

Mr. Green : OK, thanks a lot, Bye.

Receptionist: Goodbye, Mr. Green.

Vocabulary Tips

- make a reservation 예약하다(=book)(동사) reserve(예문) I'm sorry, we don't have your reservation. 죄송하지만, 손님은 예약이 안 되어 있네요.
- stay(호텔)묵다,(국가)체류하다

Hotel Room Type

- **Single Bed Room :** 1인용 침대가 1개 있는 객실
- **Double Bed Room :** 2인용 침대가 1개 있는 객실
- **Twin Bed Room :** 1인용 침대가 2개 있는 객실
- **Suite Room :** 특실을 일컬으며 보통 침실과 응접실을 갖춘 객실

Hotel Terminology

- **Front :** 호텔의 현관을 말하며, 현관에는 룸 클럭(Room Clerk), 인포메이션 클럭(Information Clerk), 키 클럭(Key Clerk), 캐셔(Cashier), 프로어 클럭(Floor Clerk) 등이 있어 현관 직무를 담당한다.
- **Reservation Confirmation :** 호텔의 시설을 사용하기 전에 예약이 확실히 되어 있는지를 확인하는 것.
- **Cancellation :** 예약취소. 약어로 CNL이라고 표기한다.
- **Extra Bed :** 객실에 정원 이상의 손님을 숙박시킬 경우 임시로 설치하는 침대로 보통 접는 식의 이동하기 쉬운 "Roll Away Bed"를 말한다.
- **Bellman :** 호텔의 프런트 부근에 있으면서 입, 퇴숙(Check-in, Check-out) 절차를 마친 숙박객의 짐운반 및 보관업무와 안내역할을 하는 호텔의 종사원. 과거에는 어린 소년이 주로 이 업무를 맡았기 때문에 Bell boy라고 불렀다. Bell Captain은 호텔 영접부에 근무하는 벨 보이(Bellman), 포터(Potter)등을 총괄하는 위치에 있는 직원.

Further Study

Types of Accommodation

apartment / bed and breakfast / campsite / caravan / chalet / country house / cruise ship / farmhouse / guest house / hostel / hotel / lodge / log cabin / motel / motorhome / mountain refuge / university hall of residence(dormitory=dorm) / villa

- caravan(美 camper)(英) 이동식 주택(승용차에 매달아 끌고 다님) a caravan site/park 이동식 주택 주차장[야영지]
- chalet 샬레(특히 스위스 산간 지방의 지붕이 뾰족한 목조 주택) 해변 휴양객용 오두막

Places to stay at while traveling

	Hotel (A place to stay with many rooms and guest services)	미국에서 호텔이라고 불리는 숙박시설은 통틀어 약 3만 개 정도라고 한다. 최고급 호텔에서 여인숙에 가까운 것까지 천차만별로, 성수기와 비수기에 따라 요금이 달라진다.
	Resort	장기간 체류하며 스포츠 또는 놀이를 즐기고 휴양하기 알맞도록 꾸민 곳을 말한다. 휴양지라고도 한다. 숙박, 스포츠 활동, 레저, 쇼핑을 한 번에 즐길 수 있게 조성하며, 어느 지역은 지역 전체가 휴양지로 조성되어 있다.
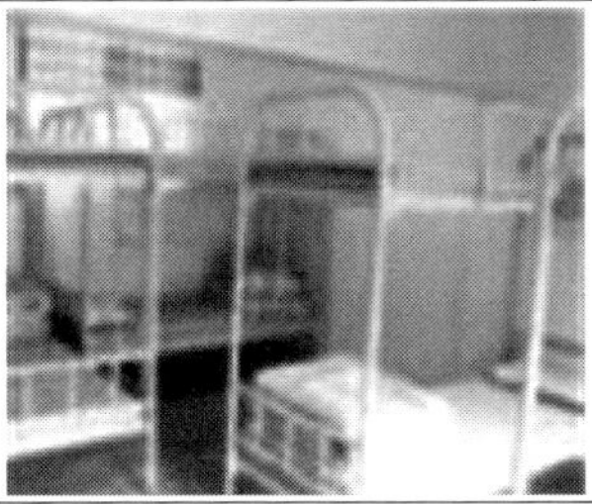	Guesthouse	게스트하우스는 침실 제공을 목적으로 여행자에게 대여할 수 있는 객실을 갖춘 숙박시설이다. 호텔은 세계어디를 가도 비슷하지만 민박(게스트하우스)는 그 나라의 일반 건축양식을 체험하고 문화를 이해하는 데 도움이 되기 때문에 또한 가격도 저렴하기에 이용한다.

	Motel	자동차 여행을 할 때 빼놓을 수 없는 숙소. 도로변에 'vacancy' 또는 'no vacancy'의 간판이 붙어 있기 때문에 차 안에서도 숙박 여부를 결정할 수 있다.
	Youth Hostel	\$20~15 정도의 저렴한 가격에 비교적 시설이 깨끗할 뿐만 아니라 국제적인 분위기로 가득 차 있어 여행정보의 장으로 활기가 넘치는 것이 장점이다.
	Cottage	"a small old house especially in the country"로서 주로 피서지의 조그만 별장을 의미함.
	YMCA / YWCA	\$30~25으로 숙박이 가능하다. 중심지의 편리한 곳에 있는 곳이 많은 대신, 건물이 낡고 서비스가 좋지 않은 것이 단점이다. 화장실과 샤워실은 공용이며, 스포츠 시설이 있다.
	Inn	고급 Motel과 비슷한 수준이며 가격은 2인 1실에 \$80~50 정도. Holiday Inn이 가장 잘 알려져 있다.

Places to live in

	Apartment	국가 또는 기업, 개인이 공동 주택을 지어 놓고 임대하여 주는 주거형태를 말함.
	House	일반적인 주택을 말함.
	Container	콘테이너를 주거용으로 변형시킨 주거형태. 주로 월세의 형태로 운영되며 가격이 매우 저렴하여 대학생들이 많이 이용함.
	Mansion	"a large house, usually belongs to a wealthy person" 부자들의 대 저택.
	Villa	주로 시골에 있는 정원이 딸려 있는 쾌적한 주택.
	Town Homes	우리나라의 연립주택과 비슷하며, 일반주택과 거의 같은데 줄줄이 붙어 있는 특징이 있고 비교적 가격이 저렴함.
	Condominium	분양되어 개인 소유로 된 공동주택

Reading about Tourism

Computer Reservation System(CRS)

A computer reservations system, or CRS, is a computerized system used to store and retrieve information and conduct transactions related to travel. Originally designed and operated by airlines, they were later extended to travel agents as a sales channel. Major CRS operations are also known as Global Distribution Systems(GDS). Many systems are now accessible to consumers through internet gateways for hotel, rental cars, and other services as well as airline tickets.

Vocabulary Tips

- store 자장하다
- retrieve 회수하다, 정보를 검색하다
- transaction 거래

CRS란 항공사 컴퓨터 예약 시스템을 말한다. 컴퓨터를 통한 전산 예약 시스템으로 전산단말기를 통해 항공좌석의 예약과 발권, 운임, 호텔, 그리고 렌트카 등, 기타 여행에 관한 종합 서비스를 제공하는 고부가가치 통신 시스템이다. 항공사는 CRS를 이용하여 현재의 고객이나 잠재적인 고객 서비스 증진과 판매원이나 예약 담당자의 수를 줄이고 항공기 좌석 탑승률을 높이는 데 목적이 있으며, 항공사와 여행사, 운송업과 관광산업을 연결하는 정보망이다.

CRS Example

Fare Basis	Airline	Booking Class	Trip Type	Fare	Cabin	Effective Date	Expiration Date	Min / Max Stay	Adv Purchase Req
TA14A0SP	DL	T	One-Way	169.00(USD)	E		02/16/11		14
TA03A0SG	DL	T	One-Way	209.00(USD)	E		02/28/11		03
UA10A0UY	DL	U	One-Way	236.00(USD)	E				10
LA10A0VY	DL	L	One-Way	251.00(USD)	E				10
LA07A0NY	DL	L	One-Way	286.00(USD)	E				07
KA07A0UY	DL	K	One-Way	326.00(USD)	E				07
QA03A0NP	DL	Q	One-Way	396.00(USD)	E				03
HA00A0NY	DL	H	One-Way	466.00(USD)	E				
UC14A0NJ	DL	U	Round-Trip	482.00(USD)	E			V / 30	14
HA00A0UY	DL	H	One-Way	616.00(USD)	E				
MA00A0RY	DL	M	One-Way	694.00(USD)	E				
MA00UPNY	DL		One-Way	1076.00(USD)	B				
BA00UPRQ	DL		One-Way	1348.00(USD)	B				
Y0	DL	Y	One-Way	1435.00(USD)	E				
YUP	DL		One-Way	1527.00(USD)	B				
F0	DL	F	One-Way	1826.00(USD)	F				
Y	DL	Y	One-Way	1889.00(USD)	E				
C	DL	C	One-Way	2213.00(USD)	B				
F	DL	F	One-Way	2766.00(USD)	F				

Hotel Front Desk — Job Description

Hotel front desk clerks make room reservations, provide information and services to guests and receive payment for services. They are employed by hotels, motels and resorts. Hotel front desk clerks perform some or all of the following duties:

- Maintain an inventory of vacancies, reservations and room assignments
- Register arriving guests and assign rooms
- Answer enquiries regarding hotel services and registration by letter, by telephone and in person, provide information about services available in the community and respond to guests' complaints
- Compile and check daily record sheets, guest accounts, receipts and vouchers using computerized or manual systems

환경을 생각하는 호텔!

GREEN CARD

Love Nature, Human's Happiness

Dear Guest,
Everyday gallons of detergents and water are used to launder sheets and towels that have been used only once. Detergents are polluting our waters. You can help in our effort to create an environmentally friendly hotel.

Please mark the box(es) below and then hang this card on your door knob.

- Do not clean my room. ☐
- Do not change my sheets. ☐

Make a difference. Save the environment
JEJU GRAND HOTEL

Did You Know . . .?

What are the most popular places to go on a package tour? It depends on where you live. The most popular places are usually the cheapest places, or ones with a very developed tourism infrastructure. In North America, it's Mexico, the Dominican Republic, Cuba, and the Caribbean, while in Europe the best deals are to Spain(Canary Islands), Portugal, Greece, Turkey, and North Africa(especially Tunisia and Egypt).

Dining in southern Europe? Spain, Portugal, Italy, and Greece, were once regarded as relatively cheap destinations, but this is changing quite fast. An average meal in Barcelona will cost you 13-17, in Rome, 18-22. Prices in all of these countries are now pretty much on-par with prices in the rest of Europe... and sometimes they're even higher.

VISUAL ENGLISH – HOSPITALITY INDUSTRY

Write the correct word(from the list below) to describe each picture:

(a) apron /(b) sandwich /(c) coaster /(d) vegetables /(e) waiter /(f) plate /(g) bowl /(h) check /
(i) meat /(j) restroom

	( )	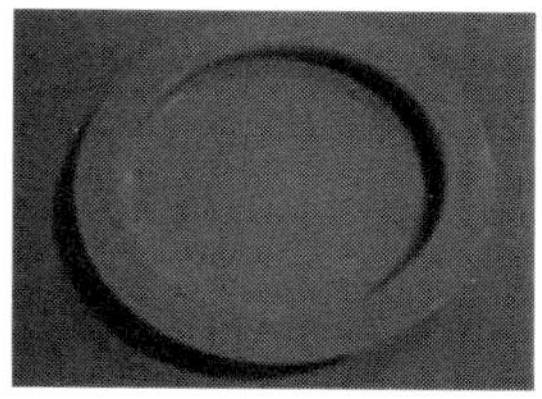	( )
	( )		( )
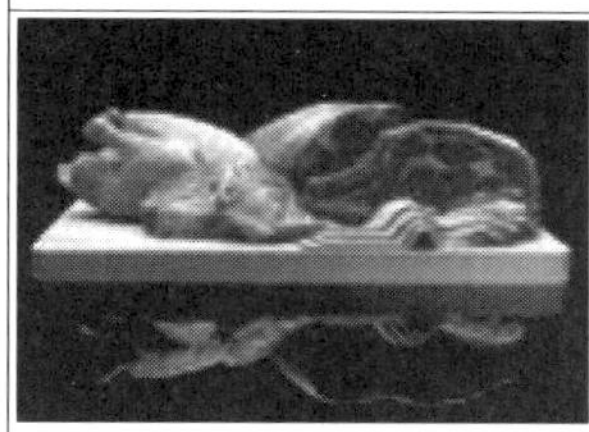	( )		( )
	( )		( )
	( )		( )

Exercise – ENGLISH FOR HOTEL EMPLOYEES : Hotel Reception/ Guest Services 1

Fill in each blank with the correct word. If both words can be used, choose the one that sounds more natural in each situation:

1. Your room hasn't been ______(clean/cleaned) yet.

2. You can check ______(in/on) from 11:00 AM.

3. Check out ______(schedule/time) is 12:00 PM.

4. Did you make your reservation ______(online/internet)?

5. Everything is in ______(good/order) = Everything is alright(= especially when talking about formal matters)

6. Do you have a restaurant on ______(promises/premises)(= in or attached to the hotel)

7. We hope you ______(enjoy/please) your stay.

8. How long will you be ______(staying/stay)?

9. I'm sorry, we don't have any rooms ______(available/rentable) that weekend.

10. Would you like me to check another ______(date/schedule) for you?

11. I'm sorry, we're all-______(books/booked)(= we have no free rooms) because of a big conference.

12. I'll need to see your passport, or some other form of ______(identity/identification).

13. We don't have room ______(servants/service).(= We don't bring food, etc. to your room)

14. The concierge will ______(show/carry) you to your room.

15. There's a ______(tiny/mini)-bar in every suite.

16. Let me know if I can be of further ______(assistance/assistant) = Let me know if there's anything else I can do to help

17. Before you arrive = ______(Prior/Previous) to your arrival

18. We also have a gym which you can use at your ______(dispersal/disposal).

Chapter 02

Check-in

Conversation : I want to check in now.

Receptionist : What can I do for you?

Ms. Barratt : I want to check in now.

Receptionist : Did you make a reservation?

Ms. Barratt : Yes, I did. My name is Jane Barratt.

Receptionist : How does your last name spell?

Ms. Barratt : B-A-R-R-A-T-T.

Receptionist : Wait a minute, ma'am. Your name is on the list. It is a single room with sea view until Saturday, is that right?

Ms. Barratt : That's right.

Receptionist : Would you fill out this registration form, please?

Ms. Barratt : Oh, yes, sure.

Receptionist : Thank you, Ms. Barratt. Could I see your passport, please?

Ms. Barratt : Uhuh, here it is.

Receptionist : Ok. Here's is your room key. You will be in Room 1202, which is on 12th floor.

Ms. Barratt : All right.

Receptionist : Enjoy your stay with us!

Ms. Barratt : Thanks!

Vocabulary Tips

- check in 호텔에서 투숙 수속을 하는 것 ↔ check out 숙박한 호텔에서 숙박료를 지급하고 퇴숙하는 것(일반적으로 12시)
- registration card(form) 숙박등록카드를 말하며, 대개 호텔의 명칭, 주소, 카드번호, 고객의 성명, 주소, 객실번호, 요금, 도착시간, 출발예정시간, 지불방법, 취급자 성명 등이 기재된다.
- fill in(out) a form 기입하다

Hotel REGISTRATION CARD **Hotel**

NAME	NATIONALITY
ADDRESS	
CITY OR TOWN	CAR REGISTRATION NO.
DATE OF ARRIVAL	DATE OF DEPARTURE
METHOD OF PAYMENT ☐ C. Card ☐ Cash ☐ Cheque	
ROOM RATE ☐ DINNER, BED & BREAKFAST ☐ BED & BREAKFAST	
NEWSPAPER ORDERED	CHECKOUT TIME 10am
SIGNATURE	ROOM NO.

Notes: Cheques must be accompanied by a current BANK card.
Credit Cards must be imprinted and signed, amount to be verified prior to departure.
Cash customers can elect to either pay in advance, or on a day to day basis.
(prior to 12 noon each day for the following days stay).

HOTEL REGISTRATION CARD

Room No.:
Reception Initials:

NAME: ....
ADDRESS: ....
SUBURB: ....
STATE: .... POST CODE: ....
TELEPHONE: ....
EMAIL: ....
CAR REGISTRATION: ....
SIGNATURE: ....
COMPANY: ....
COMPANY ADDRESS: ....
SUBURB: ....
STATE: .... POST CODE: ....
SPECIAL REQUIREMENTS: ....
....

METHOD OF PAYMENT

☐ Cash ☐ Cheque
☐ Bankcard ☐ Visa
☐ Mastercard ☐ Diners Club
☐ American Express ☐ Company
By prior arrangement only
____

DAYS OCCUPIED				ROOM TOTAL	
SUN					
MON				GST	
TUE					
WED				TOTAL	
THURS				AMT. PAID	
FRI					
SAT				AMT DUE	

Arrival Date	Arrival Time	Departure Date		Departure Time	No. of Nights
Daily Rate	No. of Guests	Adults	Children	Deposit Paid	Clerk

Hotel Terminology

- waiting list : 이미 예약이 만원되어 있는 좌석 또는 호텔 객실을 예약하기 위하여 이미 예약된 것 중 취소되는 것을 기다리고 있는 사람의 명부.
- No Show : 예약을 해놓고 아무 연락 없이 나타나지 않는 고객. 예) Restaurants are experiencing 20% no-shows at peak hours, which forces them to overbook.
- Concierge : 컨시어즈, 유럽의 호텔에 있는 직종으로서 프론트와는 달리 카운터를 두고 고객에 대한 관광안내, 여행안내, 차량예약, 우편물의 집배, 열쇠의 관리 등 그 밖의 여러 가지 서비스를 제공한다.

Further Study

Vocabulary test of hotel jobs : match the jobs with the duties

1	chambermaid	a	carries guests' bags to their rooms
2	hotel manager	b	cleans guestrooms
3	bartender	c	serves guests at the bar
4	accountant	d	manages all hotel staff
5	concierge	e	serves guests in the restaurant
6	porter	f	finds business for the hotel
7	waiter	g	gives information and helps guests
8	marketing manager	h	does the hotel's finances

Two guests check in at the reception of a hotel and put the following actions in the correct order.

a requests the guests' passports
b informs the guests of the check-out time
c asks the guests their names
d greets the guests
e advises them about the time for breakfast
f checks how to spell their surnames
g gives the room number and directions
h offers to have a porter carry their luggage

Reading about Tourism

Hotels with a difference

If you want to stay at the best hotel in the world, where should you go? Try The Oriental, Bangkok. There are more than 1,000 employees for nearly 400 rooms and suites!

What is the oldest hotel in the world? This is the Hotel Drei Konige, "Three Kings Hotel," which is in Basel, Switzerland. The first guests stayed there in 1026!

Do you want to stay in a really cool hotel? Then stay at the Icehotel in Sweden. It is made of 100% ice and snow and has to be built every year. Don't forget to bring some warm clothes!

Would you like to sleep underwater? Jules' Undersea Lodge, in Key Largo, Florida, is seven meters underwater. Watch the fish swim past your window as you relax in your air-conditioned room. Of course, you can go diving, too!

Do you have some spare cash? US$25,000 will buy you one night in the Bridge Suite of the Atlantis Hotel in the Bahamas. You get a great view of the marina, ten beautiful rooms and a personal entertainment center!

http://blog.naver.com/hjh5024

Did You Know . . .?

A selection of hotel rates in cities across the world: Vancouver(Canada) - $155 per night; Orlando(Florida) - $105 per night; Cape Town(South Africa) - $140 per night; Shanghai(China) - $120 per night; Edinburgh(Scotland) - $200 per night.

A selection of hotel rates in cities across the world: Nice(France) - $165 per night; Prague(Czech Republic) - $135 per night; Warsaw(Poland) - $130 per night; Sydney(Australia) - $160 per night; Mexico City(Mexico) - $110 per night.

A selection of hotel rates in cities across the world: Los Angeles(USA) - $145 per night; Melbourne(Australia) - $135 per night; Beijing(China) - $130 per night; Toronto(Canada) - $145 per night; Bali(Indonesia) - $145 per night.

The most expensive cities in Asia(average hotel room rates): 1) Dubai(UAE) - $245 per night; 2) Tokyo(Japan) - $185 per night; 3) Singapore - $175 per night; 4) Seoul(South Korea) - $170 per night; Hong Kong - $160 per night.

The most expensive cities in the United States and Canada(average hotel room rates): 1) New York - $285 per night; 2) Boston - $185 per night; 3) Chicago - $180 per night; 4) Miami - $165 per night; Washington - $160 per night.

VISUAL ENGLISH – HOSPITALITY INDUSTRY

Write the correct word(from the list below) **to describe each picture:**

(a) tomatoes /(b) onions /(c) garlic /(d) spoon /(f) rice /(g) bartender /(h) pasta /(i) beer /(j) potatoes /(k) wine

	(　　　　)		(　　　　)
	(　　　　)		(　　　　)
	(　　　　)		(　　　　)
	(　　　　)		(　　　　)
	(　　　　)	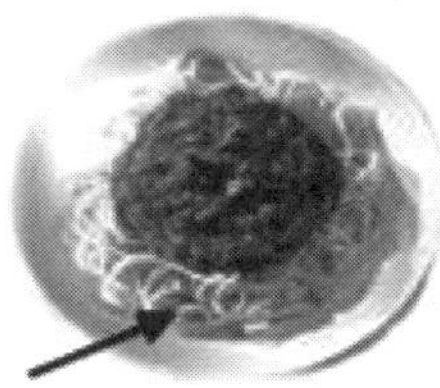	(　　　　)

Review : Hotel Vocabulary

Word	Meaning	Example sentence
adjoining rooms	two hotel rooms with a door in the centre	If you want we can book your parents in an **adjoining room**.
amenities	local facilities such as stores and restaurants	We are located downtown, so we are close to all of the **amenities**.
attractions	things for tourists to see and do	The zoo is our city's most popular **attraction** for kids.
baggage	bags and suitcases packed with personal belongings	If you need help with your **baggage** we have a cart you can use.
Bed and Breakfast =B&B	a home that offers a place to stay and a place to eat	I can book you into a beautiful **Bed and Breakfast** on the lake.
bellboy	a staff member who helps guests with their luggage	The **bellboy** will take your bags to your room for you.
book	arrange to stay in a hotel	I can **book** your family in for the weekend of the seventh.
booked	full, no vacancies	I'm afraid the hotel is fully **booked** tonight.
brochures	small booklets that provide information on the local sites and attractions	Feel free to take some **brochures** to your room to look at.
check-in	go to the front desk to receive keys	You can **check-in** anytime after four o'clock.
check-out	return the keys and pay for the bill	Please return your parking pass when you **check-out**.
complimentary breakfast	free of charge	All of our rooms have **complimentary** soap, shampoo, and coffee.
cot, rollaway bed	a single bed on wheels that folds up	If you need an extra bed, we have **cots** available.
damage charge	money a guest owes for repairs to hotel property(when caused by violent or careless acts)	We will have to add a **damage** charge for the hole you put in the wall.
(card) deposit	amount paid ahead of time to secure a reservation	You will not receive your **deposit** back if you cancel.
double bed	a bed large enough for two people	They are a family of four, so give them a room with two **double beds**.
floor	a level of the building	The swimming pool is on the main **floor**.

front desk, reception	the place where guests go to check in and out and to get information	Towels are available at the **front desk**.
guest	a person that is staying at the hotel	Our washrooms are for **guests** only.
hostel	a very inexpensive place for backpackers and travelers on a budget	In the **hostel** you probably won't get your own room.
hotel manager	person in charge at the hotel	I'll let you make your complaint to the **hotel manager.**
housekeeping, maid	staff members that clean the rooms and linen	Put a sign on the door if you want **house-keeping** to come in and change the sheets on the bed.
ice machine	a machine that automatically makes ice that guests can use to keep drinks cold	There is an **ice machine** by the elevator on all of the even numbered floors.
indoor pool	place for guests to swim inside the hotel	The heated **indoor pool** is open until 10 pm.
inn	another word for "hotel"	There's an **inn** on the other side of town that has a vacancy.
Jacuzzi, hot tub, whirl pool	a small hot pool for relaxation	Our honeymoon room has a personal **hot tub**.
king-size bed	extra large bed	A room with a **king size bed** costs an extra ten dollars a night.
kitchenette	a small fridge and cooking area	Your room has a **kitchenette** so you can pre-pare your own breakfasts and lunches.
late charge	a fee for staying past the check-out time	You will be charged a ten dollar **late charge** for checking out after 11 am.
linen	sheets, blankets, pillow cases	We will come in and change the **linens** while you are out of your room.
lobby	large open area at the front of the hotel	You can stand in the **lobby** and wait for your bus.
luggage cart	a device on wheels that guests can push their luggage on	Please return the **luggage cart** to the lobby when you are finished with it.
maximum capacity	the most amount of people allowed	The **maximum capacity** in the hot tub is ten people.
motels	accommodations that are slightly cheaper than hotels	Our **motel** is very clean and is close to the beach.
noisy	loud	The guests next to you have complained that you are being too **noisy**.

parking pass 주차증	a piece of paper that guests display in the car window while in the hotel parking lot	Display this **parking pass** in your window to show that you are a hotel guest.
pay-per-view movie	extra charge for movies and special television features	If you order a **pay-per-view** movie, the charge will appear on your bill.
pillow case	the covering that goes over a pillow	Room 201 doesn't need their sheets changed, but they requested one new **pillow case**.
queen size bed	bed with plenty of space for two people(bigger than a double)	They have a **queen size bed** so the small child can easily fit in the middle.
rate = hotel rates	cost of renting a room for a certain time period	Our **rates** change depending on the season.
reservation	a request to save a specific room for a future date	They say they made a **reservation** but it doesn't show on the computer.
room service	delivery of food or other services requested by guests	If you would like a bottle of wine, just call **room service**.
sauna	a hot room for relaxation, filled with steam	We don't recommend bringing young children into the **sauna**.
single bed	a bed for one person	The economy priced room includes one **single bed**.
sofa bed, pull-out couch	a bed built into a sofa or couch	The room contains a **sofa bed** so the room actually sleeps five.
towels	used to cover and dry the body after swimming or bathing	You can get your swimming pool **towels** at the front desk.
vacancy, vacant	available rooms	We only have one **vacancy** left, and it is for a single room.
valet	staff that parks the guests' vehicles	If you leave your car keys with us, the **valet** will park your car underground.
vending machine	a machine that distributes snacks and beverages when you insert coins	The **vending machine** on the fifth floor has chocolate bars and chips.
view	a window that offers a nice image for guests	The room is more expensive because it has a spectacular **view** of the beach.
wake up call	a morning phone call from the front desk, acts as an alarm clock	What time would you like your **wake up call**?
weight room, workout room, gym, fitness	a room that guests can use for exercise and fitness	Our **weight room** has a stair climber and a stationary bicycle.

Hotel Vocabulary Quiz

1. If you've never been to this city, you should take a look at our ______.
   a) menu　b) brochures　c) front desk　d) inn.

2. We do not have a ______. You'll have to park your car yourself.
   a) room　b) dinner　c) laundry　d) valet service

3. The room has a pull ______ , so it will sleep an extra person.
   a) off　b) over　c) out　d) on couch

4. We don't have any vacancies. We are completely ______ .
   a) vacant　b) booked　c) complimentary　d) closed

5. After your long conference you can relax in the ______ .
   a) kitchenette　b) parking lot　c) hot tub　d) front desk

6. I'll call housekeeping and ask them to bring you some fresh ______ .
   a) milk　b) dinner　c) linen　d) ice

7. If you need to do your workout we have a ______ on the third floor.
   a) weight room　b) restaurant　c) library　d) telephone

8. I'll let you voice your complaint about the rate to the ______ .
   a) housekeeper　b) valet driver　c) hotel manager　d) chef

9. Please put your used ______ in the basket and leave unused ones hanging on the rack.
   a) dishes　b) towels　c) menus　d) keys

10. If you need a midnight snack there's a ______ full of potato chips on your floor.
   a) bellboy　b) kitchenette　c) cot　d) vending machine

Chapter

03 Is there anything I can do?

Conversation : Is there anything I can do?

(Over the phone)

Front Desk : Hello, How may I help you?

Guest : Oh, this is room number 705. Can I have an extra bath towel?

Front Desk : Of course, ma'am. I'll have a room maid bring it to you right away.

Guest : Oh, thank you. One more thing. I want to go into town to do some shopping. What's the best way to go there? Is it far to walk, or should I take a taxi?

Front Desk : No, it's only ten minutes' walk and the shops are open till 10:00 PM, so you've got plenty of time.

Guest : OK. Thanks.

Front Desk : Is there anything I can do for you?

Guest : No, Thanks.

(Over the phone)

Room Service : Hello, this is room service. How can I help you?

Guest : I want to have American breakfast for two.

Room Service : May I have your name and room number, please?

Guest : I'm Michael Olsen in room 870.

Room Service : Mr. Olsen, we'll send your breakfast right away.

Guest : Can you tell me where the Kyungbok Palace is?

Front Desk : It is located in Jongro.

Guest : How can I get there?

Front Desk : You can get there by subway. Please use our hotel shuttle bus to go to the subway station. It is run by every thirty minutes in front of the hotel.

Vocabulary Tips

- **Room Maid :** 객실에서 여러 가지 서비스를 담당하는 자로 객실의 청소, 정비, 정돈 등이 주된 업무이다. Room Attendant라고도 한다.
- **Bath Towel :** 목욕 및 세면 시 사용하는 것. (towel rack)

Hotel Terminology

- **Complaint :** 고객의 불평(보통 컴프로 약자로 발음) 사항.
- **Room Service :** 객실에 투숙 중인 손님의 요청으로 식사, 음료 등을 객실에 운반하여 서브하는 호텔 식음부의 영업기능.
- **Housekeeping :** 객실관리, 고객이 사용할 호텔, 모텔 등 숙박업소의 객실을 관리하는 작업으로서 객실의 정리정돈 및 비품을 관리하여 객실을 상품의 가치가 있게끔 만드는 일련의 작업 또는 그 관리.
- **Washcloth :** 세면 및 손을 닦을 수 있는 작은 타올
- **Linen-Room :** 호텔의 린넨류를 저장하면서 필요한 제품을 Room Maid나 식당 관계자들에게 제공되어진다.

Further Study

Vocabulary test of hotel facilities : match the words to make hotel facilities and services

1	en suite	a	service
2	24-hour	b	dryer
3	quality	c	bathroom
4	spacious	d	furninshings
5	hair	e	telephone
6	direct-dial	f	room service
7	satellite	g	cleaning
8	porter	h	rooms
9	dry	i	TV

Sea Food for Culinary Art

salmon	연어	tuna	참치
cuttlefish	뼈오징어	lobster	바다가재
squid	마른 오징어	eel	장어
cavier	철갑상어 알	oyster	굴
carp	잉어	cod	대구
mackerel	고등어	scallop	가리비
flatfish	가자미	herring	청어
seaweed	해초	clam	대합
anchovy	멸치	crab	게
abalone	전복	shrimp	새우
sardine	정어리	octopus	문어
sea cucumber	해삼	snail	달팽이

Work Sheet – Dealing with Requests

Write the correct word on the line that will complete the sentence.

tour / noisy / gym / apron / get / like / early / seeds / mind / messy / change / freshly / working / room / arrange / shampoo / airline / slices / crib / replace

1. Do you _______ changing my ________ reservation?

2. Could I get a ______ put in my _________ for the baby?

3. Could we __________ rooms? Being so close to the elevator is too ______.

4. Could you _______ for a ______ to Phi Phi Island for us?

5. I'd like to ________ pancakes with bananas and peach _________ on them?

6. I would ________ extra soap and __________ left in the room.

7. Could you __________ the iron? It doesn't seem to be ___________.

8. Can I get a ________ peeled and sliced apple with the __________ removed?

9. My child is very________. Could you make sure my child wears an ________ when painting.

10. Is there any way to have the ________ open half an hour _______?

Reading about Tourism

Tourism in South Korea

Tourism in South Korea refers to the tourist industry in the Republic of Korea. In 2007, 6.4 million foreign tourists visited South Korea, making it the 36th most visited country in the world, and this number is expected to exceed 8.5 million in 2010. Most non-Korean tourists come from Japan, China, Taiwan and Hong Kong. The recent popularity of popular culture in these countries has increased tourist arrivals. Seoul is the principal tourist destination for visitors; popular tourist destinations outside of Seoul include Seorak-san national park, the historic city of Gyeongju and semi-tropical Jeju Island.

Vocabulary Tips

- refer to ~을 나타내다[~와 관련 있다]
- exceed(특정한 수 · 양을) 넘다[초과하다/초월하다]
- tourist destination 관광지
- tropical 열대 지방의, 열대의

Did You Know . . .?

It's easier than ever these days to go online and book a ticket. A good travel agent, however is still very valuable. The trick is to make yourself seem valuable to your clients by either showing that you're a) knowledgeable about different travel destinations b) able to find them the best suitable option at the best rate, and c) able to organize their whole trip from start to finish. Even with the internet, many people need professional guidance to make sure that their dream vacation turns out "dreamy", and that their romantic getaway is romantic :)

VISUAL ENGLISH – HOSPITALITY INDUSTRY

Write the correct word(from the list below) **to describe each picture:**

(a) take out box /(b) credit card swiper /(c) kitchen /(d) salt and pepper /(e) chef's jacket /(f) cookie /
(g) cocktails /(h) piece of cake /(i) fries /(j) cup of coffee

	( )		( )
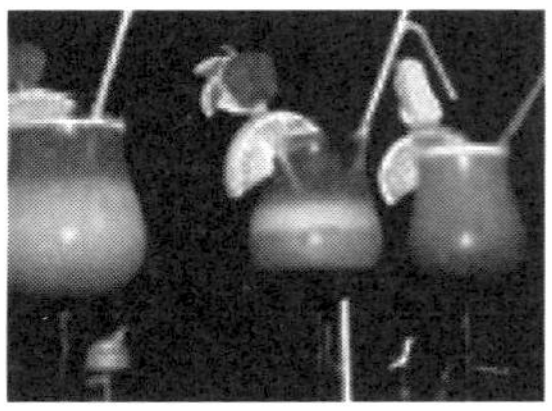	( )		( )
	( )		( )
	( )		( )
	( )		( )

Exercise – ENGLISH FOR HOTEL EMPLOYEES : Hotel Reception/ Guest Services 2

Fill in each blank with the correct word. If both words can be used, choose the one that sounds more natural in each situation:

1. A ______(concierge/counsellor) is someone who works at the reception desk.

2. I'll get one of the bellhops to take your ______(bags/baggage) to your room.

3. Someone ______(left/gave) a package for you.

4. If a room is "bigger", you can say it's more ______(spacious/spatial).

5. I'll have to ______(console/consult) with the manager = I'll have to discuss it with the manager

6. To reserve a room = To ______(book/reservation) a room

7. I can't ______(warrantee/guarantee)(= promise) that the price won't go up.

8. We have really good weekend ______(deals/offerings)(= special offers).

9. Would you like me to ______(request/call) you a taxi?

10. Breakfast is ______(inclusive/included) in your room rate.

Chapter 04

Check-Out

Conversation : Check-out

Guest : I want to check out now. Can you tell me how much my bill is?

Front Desk : Of course, sir. Just a moment, please. Here is your bill. Well, it's $120.

Guest : What's the room rate?

Front Desk : It is $120 a night but that does include buffet breakfast, sir.

Guest : Is there any other charges?

Front Desk : Yes. you used the mini bar, right? What did you have, sir?

Guest : Oh, I had some cans of beer and snack.

Front Desk : I added the price of beer and snack to the bill. How would you pay for it?

Guest : I will pay for it by credit card. Here you are.

Front Desk : Would you please sign here?

Guest : OK.

Front Desk : Thanks. I look forward to seeing you again.

Vocabulary Tips

- **bill** 영수증
- **room rate** 객실가격 cf) price 가격, fee 수수료, 요금, expense 비용
- **by credit card** 신용카드로 cf) on cash

Hotel Terminology

- **Amenity** : 고객의 편의를 꾀하고 격조 높은 서비스 제공을 위하여 객실 등 호텔에 무료로 준비해 놓은 각종 소모품 및 서비스 용품 cf) Mini-bar,
- **Housekeeper** : 호텔의 객실 청소 및 정비 책임을 맡은 자로 프론트 기술부문과 연결하여 객실을 관리 유지한다.
- **Full House :** 모든 객실이 점유되어 100%의 판매율을 나타내는 뜻.
- **stay-overs = SOs, check-outs = COs :** housekeeper들이 사용하는 용어로 '더 묵을 고객'과 '퇴숙할 고객'을 나타냄

HOTEL Invoice

HOTEL NAME:
ADDRESS:

Invoice No.:
Room No.:
Room type :

Name of the guest:
Company name:
Title:

Check in time	Check out time	Days	Amount
		Sub-total $	
		Laundry $	
		Room services $	
		Taxi $	
		Restaurant $	
		Tax	
		Total payment $	

Payment terms-Cash/Check

Cashier name:
Cashier signature:
of the guest

Signature

"Visit again"

Further Study

Reading about Tourism

* 호텔 게스트에게 설문조사를 요청하는 총지배인의 편지(객실에 비치되어 있음)

HOW WAS YOUR STAY

Dear Guests,

I really do hope that you are enjoying your stay here at Hua Ting Hotel & Towers.

Our goal at Hua Ting Hotel & Towers is to provide you with excellent service and quality facilities at great value. To help us achieve this, I would greatly appreciate a few minutes of your time to complete this questionnaire. Your comments, opinions and advice are extremely important to me, for it is only by listening to these that we are able to shape our hotel to better meet your needs in the future.

I am often told by guests that as questionnaires are rarely responded to, there is no value in completing them. For us, this is not the case – allow me to share with you how we use these questionnaires. Firstly, I respond to each personally and address issues that are raised. Secondly, we consolidate the feedback and analyse the results which enables us to focus our direction on the priority areas for improvement. Rest assured, your feedback is truly of great value.

Thank you for choosing the Hua Ting Hotel & Towers and thank you for completing this questionnaire, to which I will be responding shortly.

I look forward to welcoming you again to the Hua Ting Hotel & Towers on your next visit to Shanghai.

Yours Sincerely,

Quin Chen

General Manager
Hua Ting Hotel & Towers

Vocabulary Tips

- facilities 시설
- complete 완성하다
- questionnaire 설문지
- responded to -에 응답하다
- consolidate 굳히다, 강화하다, 통합하다
- address issues 문제들을 해결하다
- Rest assured(that ~)(자신이 하는 말을 강조하여)(~임을) 확신해도[믿어도] 된다
- General Manager : 총지배인(GM)

Reading about Tourism

* 호텔 게스트에게 부탁하는 설문조사 문항

Please rate our service from the following.

SERVICE STAFF : Doorman, Bell Team, Reception, Concierge, Telephone Operator, Room Attendants, Laundry and/or Valet Service, Guest Relations, Business Center

POOR AVERAGE EXCELLENT

① ② ③ ④ ⑤

□ □ □ □ □

Guest Room : Cleanliness, Adequacy of room lighting, Temperature control. Decor of room, Mattress comfort, Pillow comfort, Bathroom amenities

POOR AVERAGE EXCELLENT

① ② ③ ④ ⑤

□ □ □ □ □

Recreation Facilities : Swimming Pool, Fitness Center

POOR AVERAGE EXCELLENT

① ② ③ ④ ⑤

□ □ □ □ □

Other : How was our overall service? / How was the warmth of our welcome? / Please evaluate for money?

POOR AVERAGE EXCELLENT

① ② ③ ④ ⑤

□ □ □ □ □

Food & Beverage : Quality and Service of Coffee Shop(Breakfast, Lunch, Dinner), **Chinese Restaurant, Other Restaurant, Bar or Lobby Lounge, Room Service, Entertainment**

POOR		AVERAGE		EXCELLENT
①	②	③	④	⑤
□	□	□	□	□

Other Comments

Ⓐ Is there anything you would like changed in your room? ________

Ⓑ Number of visits to Shanghai a year? _______

Ⓒ Was this your first stay at the hotel? □ Yes, □ No

Ⓓ What influenced your choice of our hotel? □ Reputations □ Company □ Travel Agent □ Advertisements □ Previous experience □ Other/Internet

Ⓔ If your travel plans bring you back to Shanghai, will you return to our hotel?
□ Yes □ No

Ⓕ Are there any employees whom you felt really went out of their way to make your stay more enjoyable? ________________

Name: _______ Room number: ________ Dates of Stay: _________

Did You Know . . .?

Ecotourism is short for ecological tourism. It's a type of tourism that focuses on exploring the plant and animal life of a region, as well as learning the local customs. It appeals to socially and environmentally conscious individuals. What are the most popular destinations for ecotourism? Alaska, Costa Rica, the Amazon region, Antarctica, Borneo, Botswana, the Blue Mountains(New South Wales, Australia), The Galapagos Islands(off the coast of Ecuador), and the Himalaya Mountains.

VISUAL ENGLISH : HOSPITALITY INDUSTRY

Write the correct word(from the list below) to describe each picture:

(a) beauty mask /(b) robe /(c) beach umbrella /(d) eye shade /(e) slot machine /(f) bathtub /(g) dealer /
(h) massage /(i) purse /(j) chips

	( )	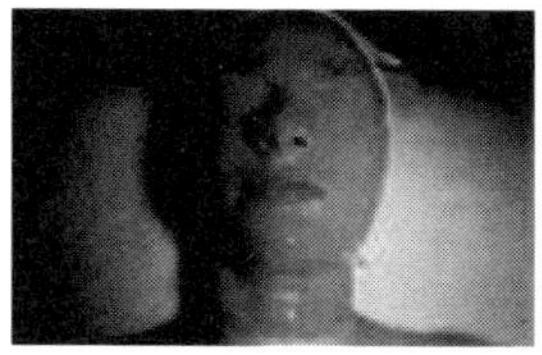	( )
	( )		( )
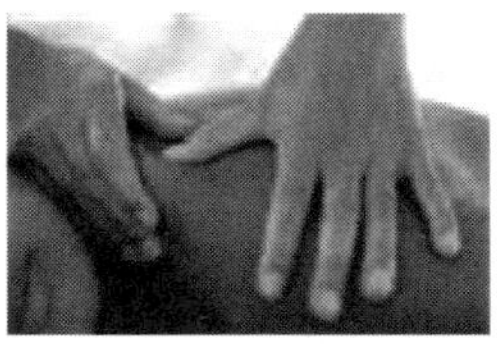	( )		( )
	( )		( )
	( )		( )

Exercise – ENGLISH FOR HOTEL EMPLOYEES : Hotel Reception/ Guest Services 3

This exercise is for hotel concierges, bellhops, reception desk workers, managers, etc. Fill in each blank with the correct word. If both words can be used, choose the one that sounds more natural in each situation:

1. The rate for that room is ______(slightly/lightly)(= a little) higher.

2. I can ______(assist/assess)(= help) you with this.

3. Is there a ______(trouble/problem) with your room?

4. Are you having ______(trouble/problem) opening the door?

5. We offer ______(washing/laundry) service for our guests.

6. This service is ______(given/provided) as part of your room rate.

7. Breakfast is not included in the price. You will have to pay ______(extra/money) for it.

8. We offer 24-______(hour/hours) room service.

9. The word "amenities" refers to "comforts" or ______(conveniences/conventions). These may include a pool, a sauna, a restaurant, etc.

10. We have an ______(indoor/inside) pool for our guests.

Hotel Review

호텔 reservation(예약)은 일찍 하는 것이 좋다. 예약이 꽉 차서(booked up) 방을 못 구할 수도 있기 때문이다. 전화로 예약을 할 경우 호텔 예약 담당자가 도착시간, 숙박일시, party(일행)의 수와 single(싱글), double(더블), twin(트윈) 등의 원하는 객실 종류를 묻는다. 그리고 smoking room(흡연층 객실)과 no-smoking room(금연층 객실) 중에서 원하는 쪽을 물은 뒤 손님에게 room rate(방값)을 알려주고 손님의 예약 여부를 묻게 된다. 이때 본인의 이름을 말하고 방을 잡아두면 된다. 이때 reservation number(예약번호)도 함께 받게 되는데, 예약 확인이나 취소 시에 필요하므로 잘 적어두어야 한다.

호텔에 도착하면 먼저 front desk(프런트)로 가서 check-in을 해야 한다. receptionist(접수계원)에게 본인 이름과 예약한 객실 종류를 말하고 registration card(숙박 카드)를 작성하면 객실 열쇠를 받게 된다. 짐이 많은 경우에는 doorman(도어맨)이나 bellboy(벨보이)의 도움을 받는다. 물론 이들에게 service charge(봉사료)인 tip을 주어야 한다. 팁은 몇 달러 이내에서 해결하면 된다.

웬만한 규모의 호텔에는 호화로운 거실과 침실이 있는 suite(스위트)가 있으며, 대규모 capacity(수용능력)을 갖춘 conference room(회의실), sauna(사우나), fitness center(건강 센터) 등 갖가지 accommodation(숙박시설)이 갖추어져 있다. 객실에 있는 텔레비전을 시청할 때는 유료 채널과 무료 채널이 있으므로 미리 확인해야 한다. 장거리 전화와 국제 전화가 아니라면 객실 전화를 호텔 교환을 거치지 않고 무료로 사용할 수 있다. 또한 restaurant(레스토랑), lounge(라운지)나 meeting room(소회의실)이 있으므로 약속 장소로도 이용할 수 있다. 호텔에서 사람을 찾을 때는 방송으로 사람을 찾는(page) 방법을 사용하기도 한다.

보통 하루에 한 번 정도씩 maid(호텔 여급)가 방에 들어와 maid service(객실 청소 서비스)를 한다. 팁은 침대 위에 놓아두면 된다. 그리고 음식 등을 객실로 갖다 주는 room service도 제공되는데 대부분 음식값과 함께 팁을 주는 것이 일반적이다. 다음날 아침 일찍 일어날 필요가 있을 때 wake-up call(모닝콜) 서비스를 신청하면 원하는 시간에 교환이 객실로 전화를 해서 잠을 깨워준다. 외출할 때는 프런트에 객실 열쇠를 맡기거나 휴대할 수 있다. 외출 시 valuables(귀중품)는 직접 소지하거나 프런트의 safety box(귀중품 보관함)에 보관하도록 한다.

- accommodation 숙박시설
- bellboy 벨보이(=bellhop, bellman)
- booked up 예약이 모두 된(Ex. All the hotels in the area are booked up weeks in advance.)
- capacity 수용 능력
- check-in 체크인, 투숙
- check-out 체크아웃, 퇴숙
- conference room 회의실
- doorman 도어맨
- double room ; 침대 한 개가 있는 2인용 객실
- fitness center 운동시설
- key deposit 열쇠 예치금
- lobby 로비
- lounge 라운지
- maid(호텔의) 여급
- maid service 객실 청소 서비스
- meeting room 소회의실
- non-smoking room 금연층 객실
- page(구내 방송이나 삐삐로)호출하다
- party 일행 ; a group of people who are involved in an activity together
- receptionist 접수계원
- registration card 숙박카드
- restaurant 레스토랑
- reservation 예약
- reservation number 예약번호
- reserve 예약하다
- room rate 방값, 숙박료
- room service 룸 서비스
- safety box 귀중품 보관함
- sauna 사우나
- service charge 봉사료, 팁(=tip)
- single 싱글룸 ; 1인용 객실
- suite 스위트 ; a set of connected rooms in a hotel
- twin 트윈룸 ; 싱글 침대 두 개가 있는 2인용 객실
- valuables 귀중품
- wake-up call 모닝콜

Chapter 05 A Table for Two

Conversation 1 : A Table for Two

Waitress : Good evening, sir. How many in your party?

Guest : Yes. I want to have a table for two.

Waitress : Did you make a reservation?

Guest : Yes. I made a reservation under the name of John Peterson.

Waitress : Wait a minute, sir. We have your reservation. Please come this way. Would you like this table?

Guest : Yes. It is nice.

Waitress : May I hang up your clothes?

Guest : Yes, please. Thanks a lot.

Waitress : Can I take your order now?

Guest : No. I am not ready.

Waitress : All right, sir. I'll be back in a minute. Take your time.

(A moment later)

Guest : What is today's special food?

Waitress : Today's special food is bulgogi.

Guest : What is it?

Waitress : It is seasoned beef cooked on the grill.

Guest : It is delicious?

Waitress : Yes it is. Many foreign visitors like it.

Guest : Okay, I'll have bulgogi.

Vocabulary Tips

- How many in your party? = How many? Party of what?
- hang up 걸다
- seasoned 양념한

Conversation 2 : Enjoy your meal.

Waiter: Welcome to Antico's. Here are your menus. Today's special is grilled salmon. I'll be back to take your order in a minute.

. . .

Waiter: Are you ready to order?

Customer 1: I'd like the seafood spaghetti.

Waiter: And you?

Customer 2: I'll have a hamburger and fries.

Waiter: Would you like anything to drink?

Customer 1: I'll have a coke, please.

Waiter: And for you?

Customer 2: Just water, please.

Waiter: OK. So that's one seafood spaghetti, one hamburger and fries, one coke, and one water. I'll take your menus.

. . .

Waiter: Here is your food. Enjoy your meal.

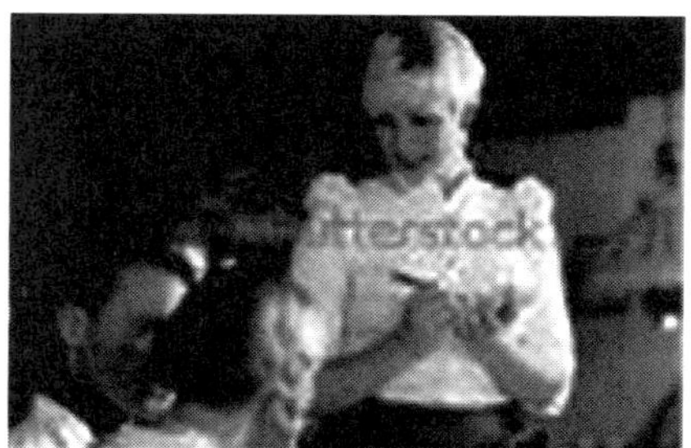

. . .

Waiter: How was everything?

Customers 2: Delicious, thanks.

Waiter: Would you like anything for dessert?

Customer 1: No, just the bill please.

Hotel Terminology

- **Turndown Service :** 이브닝 서비스(Evening Service)로 침대 덮개를 벗기고 고객의 취침을 위해 준비하거나 객실을 정리한 뒤, 사용한 비품과 린넨을 교체시키는 것을 말한다.
- **Adjoining Room :** 인접한 두 객실 사이에 통로가 없이 이어진 객실.
- **Mini Bar :** 고객의 편의를 위하여 간단하게 주류나 음료를 사용할 수 있도록 객실에 준비되어 있는 작은 바.
- **Luggage Chair :** 고객의 짐을 놓을 수 있게 만든 의자.

Further Study

Ways of Cookings

boil(끓이기, 삶기) - bake(빵, 과자를 불에 직접 대지 않고 굽는 것) - fry(기름에 튀기는 것) - roast(기름칠을 하여 굽거나 볶는 것) - stuff(빽빽히 채워 넣다) - grill, broil(생선, 고기를 직접 불에 쬐어 석쇠에 굽는 것) - poach(끓는 액체에 넣고 데치기) - stew(은근한 불로 끓이기, 찌기) - smoke(훈제하다) - mash(짓이기다) - mince(잘게 저미다) - marinate(양념에 담가 절이다)

식사를 할 때 나오는 계란요리 종류

1. fried egg(프라이한 계란)
   ⓐ sunny-side up : 계란의 한쪽 면만 프라이한 요리
   ⓑ over easy : 계란의 양쪽 면을 프라이한 요리(노른자는 익히지 않음)
   ⓒ over medium : 계란의 흰자를 완전히 프라이하고 계란의 노른자를 살짝 익힌 것
   ⓓ over hard : 흰자와 노른자를 완전히 프라이한 것
2. scrambled egg : 우유를 섞어 휘저은 계란을 팬에 휘저으며 요리한 계란
3. boiled egg : 삶은 계란(soft boiled egg, medium boiled egg, hard boiled egg)
4. omelet : 계란말이

steak의 종류 및 기타 고기류

1. tenderloin steak(안심)
2. sirloin steak(등심)
3. porter house steak(안심과 그 주위 뼈를 자른 아주 큰 스테이크)
4. T-bone steak(T자 모양 steak)
5. veal(송아지 고기)
6. calf(어린 송아지 고기)
7. pork(돼지고기)

8. lamb(양고기)
9. chicken(닭고기)
10. turkey(칠면조)

Reading about Tourism

Pub?

Pub lunches are very popular in Britain. Families often eat in pubs at weekends and
many people spend their lunch break from work in the pub. The choice and quality of pub food varies greatly but in general it is good and prices are reasonable. Some pubs also serve food in the evening which is cheaper than in restaurant.

Did You Know . . .?

What are the most popular places to go on a package tour? It depends on where you live. The most popular places are usually the cheapest places, or ones with a very developed tourism infrastructure. In North America, it's Mexico, the Dominican Republic, Cuba, and the Caribbean, while in Europe the best deals are to Spain(Canary Islands), Portugal, Greece, Turkey, and North Africa(especially Tunisia and Egypt).

The United States attracts about 45 million visitors per year. Most of these come from neighboring Canada and Mexico(15 and 9 million respectively). A lot of tourists also visit from Japan(5 million), The UK(3 million), and Germany(2 million).

There was recently a survey done on the most disappointing tourist spots(according to travelers), and here they are: 1) The Eiffel Tower(Paris), 2) The Mona Lisa painting in the Louvre(Paris), 3) Times Square(New York City), 4) Las Ramblas(Barcelona), and 5) The Statue of Liberty(New York). All of these spots failed to impress a lot of travelers :)

VISUAL ENGLISH : HOSPITALITY INDUSTRY

– Food and Beverage

Write the correct word(from the list below) to describe each picture:

(a) cutlery /(b) glass /(c) trays /(d) fork /(f) knife /(g) napkin /(h) menu /(i) straw /(j) tablecloth /(k) pitcher

	( )		( )
	( )		( )
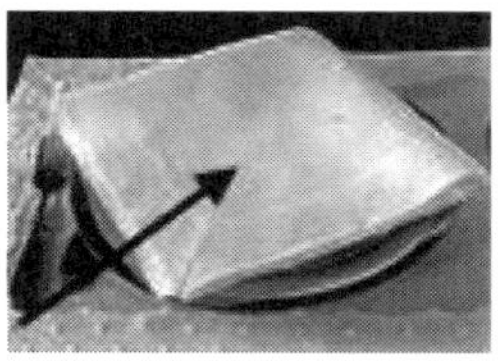	( )		( )
	( )		( )
	( )		( )

Exercise – ENGLISH FOR RESTAURANT STAFF/EMPLOYEES

Fill in each blank with the correct word. If both words can be used, choose the one that sounds more natural in each situation:

1. Are you ______(prepared/ready) to order?

2. The soup of the ______(day/special) is "Cream of Broccoli."

3. Our ______(specials/deals) are listed on the board.

4. I ______(recommend/request) the vegetarian chili.

5. We can ______(substitute/subtract) the bacon for cheese, if you like.
(=We can give you cheese instead of bacon)

6. I'll be right ______(back/return) with your drinks.

7. This meal consists of three courses - soup, the ______(main/prime) course, and dessert.

8. The chicken ______(comes/arrives) with your choice of rice or potatoes.

9. I'm sorry, we're fully/completely ______(booked/baked).
(=we have no free tables) right now.

10. If you would like, you can wait at the bar until a table ______(opens/comes) up.(=becomes available)

English for Food and Drink Staff

Are you a chef, bartender, or waiter/waitress working in a tourist spot? Maybe you're a student who wants to work part-time in a restaurant while you go to school abroad. Whatever the case may be, you will come across many English customers and staff members in the food and beverage industry. These pages are designed to help people who are employed, or looking for work in many different areas of the hospitality industry, including in the kitchen, on the floor, or behind the bar. You will learn helpful English vocabulary and expressions that will allow your guests to enjoy their dining experience and help you to communicate with your fellow staff members. Studying and practicing Food and Beverage English and gaining a better understanding of the industry may even help you find a job. Do the exercises and take the quizzes to test your knowledge and understanding.

F&B Vocabulary

Note: Many English words and expressions about food come directly from French. This is why some words about food are written with an accent(for example: à la carte). However, you may also see such words written without accent.

Vocabulary *part of speech*	**Meaning**	**Example sentence**
à la carte *adjective*	without a side dish	Is it possible to get the steak **à la carte**? I don't eat potatoes.
à la mode *adjective*	with ice cream	Would you like your apple pie **à la mode**?
alcohol, liquor *noun*	a distilled liquid such as rum or whiskey	This beer has 5% **alcohol**.
all you can eat *adjective*	customers pay one fee and can eat as much as they wish	These are **all you can eat** fries, so let me know if you want more.
appetizer *noun*	small snack before a meal	Would you like some garlic bread or another **appetizer** to start?
appetizing *adjective*	looks pleasing to eat	I'm afraid these pancakes don't look very **appetizing**.
apron *noun*	a cloth covering worn over the clothes while cooking	Remove your **apron** before you come out to the dining room.
awful(taste) *adjective*	very bad taste	The customer said that her pasta was **awful**.
bar *noun*	place in an establishment where people go to get a drink(especially alcoholic drinks)	If you sit up at the **bar** you don't have to order any food.

barbeque *noun/verb*	southern style of cooking over a grill	The **barbeque** wings are our specialty.
barstool *noun*	tall seats that customers use at the bar	The guest fell off his **barstool** before he even ordered a drink.
bartender *noun*	staff member that mixes, pours, and serves alcoholic beverages	I do part-time work as a **bartender** in a local pub.
beverage *noun*	drink	Can I bring you some **beverages** while you look at the menus?
bill, cheque, check *noun*	the slip of paper that tells the customer how much to pay	Table 3 would like you to bring them their **cheque**.
black coffee *adjective + noun*	coffee without any milk	Should I bring some cream, or do you take your coffee **black**?
boil *verb*	style of cooking that involves placing food in a deep pot of extremely hot water	We usually **boil** the potatoes first so that they will cook faster.
book off *verb*	mark a day that you cannot work	I need to **book** off the first week of May.
booster seat *noun*	a plastic unit that fits on top of a chair to help small children reach the table	Will your child be needing a **booster seat** today?
booth/bench *noun*	type of seating in which people sit side by side on a cushioned area	We'd prefer a **booth** if you have one available.
booze *noun(idiom)*	alcohol	You've been into the **booze** already, haven't you?
bottle opener *noun*	a device used for opening beer bottles that don't twist off	All of the servers keep **bottle openers** on their keychains.
bread basket *noun*	slices of bread and butter served before and with a meal	I'll bring you a **bread basket** to hold the kids down until dinner.
breaded *adjective*	rolled and cooked in bread crumbs	The shrimp is **breaded** in our homemade batter.
buffet *noun*	self-serve tables of food that are set out for the customer to pick and choose from	The plates and everything you need are up at the **buffet**.
burnt *adjective*	overcooked to the point of turning black	The toast is **burnt** around the edges.
buspan *noun*	rubber tub used for collecting dirty dishes	The **buspan** is stacked so high it's too heavy for me to carry.
busboy, busser *noun*	a person who helps out in a restaurant(especially clearing and setting tables)	Ask the **busboy** to help you bring out all of the food.

cash *noun*	paper money payment	I don't have any **cash**. Do you accept Visa?
cash out *verb*	counting and submitting the payment of all of the customers bills at the end of one's shift	Don't forget to include any coupons from tonight when you **cash out** later.
cashier *noun*	staff member responsible for collecting customer's money at the front of an establishment	We don't have a **cashier**; you have to pay your server.
charge *verb*	to add a fee	I will have to **charge** you an extra dollar to add ice cream.
check on *verb*	make sure the guests are satisfied	You should always **check on** your guests about two minutes after you serve the meal.
chef *noun*	staff member who is professionally trained to prepare food	Our head chef is one of the best cooks in town.
clear *verb*	remove finished or unused items from a table	You need to **clear** this table and set it for four.
cocktail *noun*	an alcoholic drink with juice	Would anyone care for a **cocktail** on this warm sunny day?
coffee maker *noun*	machine that dispenses coffee into a glass container for pouring	You need to teach the new waitress how to operate the **coffee maker**.
coffee round *noun*	an offering of coffee and refills around a section of a restaurant	Let's ask the busboy to do a **coffee round** while we take a smoke break.
combo, combination *noun*	mixture	The **combo** platter has veggies, ribs, and chicken fingers.
comment card *noun*	a piece of paper that customers are given to record their dining experience	When she asked for a **comment card** I knew she was going to complain about the food.
complaint *noun*	a problem with service or food	The guest brought his **complaint** to the manager.
condiments *noun*	types of sauces that are added for flavouring(i.e. mustard)	All of the **condiments** you should need are on the table.
cook *verb/noun*	prepare and heat food until it is ready to serve	The guest says that this chicken isn't **cooked** enough.
corkscrew *noun*	tool for removing the cork from the top of a wine bottle.	You will need to learn how to work a **corkscrew** before you start bartending.
counter *noun*	flat area often used for placing dishes on or preparing food	I left one of the salads on the kitchen **counter** by mistake.

coupon *noun*	a slip of paper that offers the customers a discounted rate	Your **coupon** is only valid for food, not for alcoholic drinks.
complimentary *adjective*	free of charge	The desserts are **complimentary** because the dinner took so long.
creamer *noun*	small plastic container of cream for coffee	Will you need more than two **creamers** for your coffee?
credit card *noun*	a plastic card that allows people to pay for something later	You forgot to sign your **credit card** slip.
customer, guest *noun*	person who goes to an establishment to be served	It is our policy that the **customer** is always right.
customer service *noun*	treatment of guests	Our restaurant got the award for having the best **customer service** this year.
cutlery, silverware, utensils *noun*	tools for eating with(fork, knife, spoon)	In a fine dining restaurant the staff has to polish the **silverware**.
cut off *verb*	stop serving a customer any more alcohol	I **cut off** the man with the beard because he'd had too much to drink.
debit *noun*	use bank card to pay directly from bank account	Can we pay by **debit** here, or do you only take credit cards?
deep fried *adjective*	cooked in a large pot of oil	Most of the appetizers on our menu are **deep fried**.
defrost, thaw *verb*	remove frozen food from the freezer to prepare	Don't forget to **defrost** some pies for tomorrow.
delicious *adjective*	very good taste	The cookies were so **delicious** they were gone in half an hour.
delivery *noun*	food brought to the home	Do you have **delivery** or do we have to come in to eat?
designated driver *adjective + noun*	person in a party who agrees not to consume alcohol in order to drive everyone home safely	Is there a **designated driver** in your party or are you taking a taxi?
dessert *noun*	sweet treat after a meal	I think we're too full to have **dessert** tonight.
dessert tray *noun*	a plate of all of the desserts that customers can view and order from	I'll bring the **dessert tray** around and see if I can tempt any of you with a slice of cake or pie.
dirty dishes *adjective + noun*	plates that customers are finished with	I'll just clear these **dirty dishes** and make some room for you.

discount *noun*	at a cheaper cost	We got a **discount** because we are regular customers.
dishpit *noun*	area in the restaurant where the dirty dishes are placed.	Jody is not going to want to go into the **dishpit** today.
dishwasher *noun*	the staff member/machine that washes the dirty dishes	Can you bring the **dishwasher** these pans to clean?
doggie bag *noun*	unfinished food that is packed up for the customer to take home	I can't finish my steak, but I'll take a **doggie bag**.
double *noun*	two shots of alchohol in one drink	Make that a **double** in a tall glass, please.
draft *noun*	beer from a keg that pours out of a tap	We have a selection of local beers on **draft**.
dressing *noun*	liquid topping for salads	Would you like Italian or French **dressing**?
dry *adjective*	no sauce	I'll have **dry** toast with two eggs.
entrée, main course *noun*	the largest part of a meal(after appetizer, before dessert)	The **entrées** are after the lunch specials on page 6 of the menu.
fast-food *noun*	an eatery that offers quick inexpensive food	We don't provide table service. This is a **fast-food** restaurant.
fine dining *noun*	a very expensive eating establishment	The waiters wear bowties because it's a **fine dining** restaurant.
float *noun*	small amount of cash used to make change at the beginning of a server or bartender's shift	I need a roll of quarters for my **float**.
free refills *adjective + noun*	beverages that can be filled again without any cost	Have all of the soda you want; it's free **refills here**.
fry *verb*	cook over an element in oil	Don't **fry** the vegetables too long or they will go soggy.
garnish *noun/verb*	food that is added to a plate for appearance or colour(i.e. parsley or fruit)	Don't forget to **garnish** all of the entrees that go out.
glassware *noun*	group of drinking glasses	Make sure the **glassware** doesn't have any spots before you put it away.
gloves(plastic) *noun*	covering for the hands to prevent the spread of germs	Whenever you are handling food make sure you are wearing **gloves**.

gratuity/tip *noun*	extra money given as a thank you for service	When we have a large party we're allowed to add a 15% **gratuity** to the bill.
greet *verb*	say hello and welcome customers to the establishment	Your priority as a hostess is to **greet** the guests at the door with a smile.
grill *noun/ verb*	cooking over iron slats that allow for oil and fat to drop down	The healthiest way to prepare meat is on a **grill**.
hairnet *noun*	a covering worn on the head while preparing food	If you don't want to wear a hat, you can wear a **hairnet**.
happy hour *noun*	short amount of time when alcoholic drinks are on sale	We're expecting a rush because it's almost **happy hour**.
highball *noun*	alcohol served with soda	Our **highballs** are on for half price today.
highchair *noun*	a tall chair with a plastic tray designed for a baby	The party is for ten plus a **highchair**.
hold *verb*	leave off/without	I'll take a hamburger, **hold** the bun.
homemade *adjective*	made from a recipe	We serve the best **homemade** soup in town.
host, hostess *noun*	staff member in charge of greeting and seating customers in a restaurant	Please wait and the **hostess** will seat you.
ingredients *noun*	all of the different foods that are combined in a recipe	I'll check the **ingredients** to make sure there aren't any nuts.
kettle *noun*	pot for boiling water for tea	I'll put the **kettle** on and make some fresh tea.
last call *noun*	the last chance for a person to get an alcoholic drink before the establishment closes	We'll have two more screwdrivers for **last call**.
lemon, lime wedge *noun*	a small segment of lemon or lime put on the rim of a glass	I'd like a **lemon** wedge for my ice water please.
lineup *noun /verb*	a number of people waiting for something	Is this the **lineup** to pay or get seated?
liqueur *noun*	alcohol that has a syrupy/sweet taste	Can I offer you a coffee **liqueur** to go with your dessert?
make change *verb + noun*	give customers money back from a payment	We can **make change** if all you have is large notes.
manager *noun /adjective*	person in charge of a section of a restaurant	I'd like to speak to the floor **manager** about the service.

melt *verb*	warm to soften(i.e. cheese/butter)	First, **melt** two tablespoons of butter in the microwave.
menu *noun*	a booklet of all of the food that can be ordered	Do you have a children's **menu** we could see?
microwave *noun*	a small appliance that heats and cooks food quickly	We can heat your dinner in the **microwave** if you like.
mild *adjective*	not spicy	I'd like a half dozen **mild** chicken wings.
nightclub *noun*	establishment where adults go to dance and drink alcoholic beverages	If you work at the **nightclub** you will have to stay until 2 AM.
non alcoholic beverage *adjective + noun*	a drink that resembles a certain drink without the alchohol	Can I order a **non alcoholic** beer?
notepad *noun*	paper that a server uses to write down orders	Just let me grab my **notepad** and I'll take your order.
on the rocks *preposition + noun*	on ice	I'll take a whiskey **on the rocks**.
on the side *preposition + noun*	request for a food item to NOT be put on top of another food item	For the nachos, can we have the sour cream **on the side**?
order *verb/noun*	make a request to a server	Is everyone ready to **order** lunch now?
over charge *verb*	give a customer a bill that is too high(by mistake)	I think you **over charged** us for our drinks; we only had one each.
pack up *verb*	put in a take-out container for the customer to bring home	Would you like me to **pack up** the rest of that pizza?
party *noun*	group of people at or waiting for a table	A **party** of twelve just walked in without a reservation.
patio *noun*	outdoor seeating	We closed the **patio** because it looks like it's going to rain.
paycheque *noun*	money given to the staff every week or two	You'll get a **paycheque** every other Monday.
pitcher, jug *noun*	a container with a spout to pour water, beer, or other beverages out of	We'll take a **pitcher** of beer with four glasses.
portion *noun/verb*	a separate amount of food	The chicken fingers are already **portioned** in the freezer.
pour *verb*	dispense liquid from a container	Can I **pour** you folks another glass of water?

prepare *verb*	get food ready	The servers have to **prepare** the salads themselves.
pub *noun*	establishment that specializes in casual food and alcoholic beverages	I can wear whatever I want when I work at the **pub**.
punch clock and punch card *noun*	a machine that staff members place a card into when they begin and finish a work shift	I don't want staff members hanging around the **punch clock**.
punch in, out *verb*	put a card in the punch clock to mark the time you start and end a shift	You can **punch out** as soon as you finish sweeping the floors.
punch something in *verb*	enter an order into a computer system	I'm going to **punch in** a large order now, so get ready.
rare *adjective*	cooked meat that is pink inside	This steak is too **rare** for me to eat.
recipe *noun*	list of ingredients and instructions for preparing a certain type of food	Our chef is so talented that he almost never bothers with a **recipe**.
regulars *noun*	people who come into an establishment often	You can give the **regulars** a complimentary drink from time to time.
reservation *noun*	a request to have a table saved for a certain amount of people	We don't take any **reservations**; it's first come first served here.
restrooms *noun*	place for people to use a toilet and wash hands	The **restrooms** are to your left and down the stairs.
roll-up *noun*	a set of cutlery wrapped in a napkin	Before we punch out we have to prepare enough **roll-ups** for the night shift.
rush *noun*	a large amount of customers arriving at the same time	We always have a **rush** after church on Sundays.
rush *noun /verb*	prepare quickly for a certain reason	Can you put a **rush** on this spaghetti; I forgot to punch it in.
sauce *noun*	liquid flavouring added to food	What kind of **sauce** would you like on your ice cream, butterscotch or chocolate?
schedule *noun/ verb*	a notice of the time and date each staff member has to work in a certain period of time	If you want to book off a day, let me know before I make the **schedule**.
seasoning *noun*	dry flavouring added to food	He wants the chicken plain without any **seasoning**.
self-serve **adjective**	the customers bring their own food items to the table and do not pay for service	We have a buffet on, so it's **self-serve** for lunch.

senior's discount *noun*	a reduced price for people over a certain age(i.e. over 65)	We have a **senior's discount** of 25% off on Mondays.
separate cheques *adjective + noun/verb +noun*	a different bill for each member/group sitting at a table	We asked for **separate cheques** but it all came on one bill.
serve *verb*	look after a customer, bring items to a customer	Is there someone in charge of **serving** out on the patio?
set *verb*	get a table ready with items such as cutlery and glassware	I need you to clear and **set** table five for a party of eight.
shade *noun*	place outside that is not in the sun	We'd like to sit on the patio if there is any **shade**.
shot *noun*	one ounce of alcohol served in a small glass(shot glass)	Let's do a **shot** to get this party started.
shooter *noun*	an ounce of alcohol and juice combined	Is there a **shooter** that has orange juice in it?
side dish *noun*	choice of food that goes with a main meal	The two **side dishes** are mashed potatoes or french fries.
sour *adjective*	acid or fermented taste	I think the milk has gone **sour** from sitting out of the fridge too long.
sous chef *noun*	staff member who works under and assists the main chef	Our **sous chef** is leaving to become the head chef at another restaurant.
specials *noun*	items that were prepared particularly for a certain day and are usually at a reduced price	Would you like to hear the **specials** before you decide on lunch.
specialty *noun*	food item that a restaurant is popular for	Homemade fish and chips is our **specialty**.
spicy *adjective*	hot flavour	Any item with three chilies beside it means that the dish is very **spicy**.
stay *verb*	to eat in the restaurant	Are these coffees to go or to **stay**.
stir, mix *verb*	spin round and round with a spoon	**Stir** the soup for a few minutes before you serve it.
straw *noun*	long hollow plastic stick for drinking out of	Can I please get a **straw** for my ice tea?
straight up *adjective*	alcoholic drink without any mix or ice	He always has a **straight up** glass of rum after his meal.
substitute *verb*	replace one item for another	Can I **substitute** the carrots for corn?

supervisor *noun*	staff member in charge of watching over things and dealing with problems	When I'm not here George will be your **supervisor**.
sweet *adjective*	taste with a lot of sugar	If you like **sweet** things, you'll love our chocolate cheesecake.
take-out *adjective/verb*	food that is packed up and eaten at home	You can either eat in or order food to **take-out**.
two-minute check *noun*	a visit to a table approximately two minutes after the food has been served to check for satisfaction	Don't forget to do your **two-minute check** to make sure the steak is cooked properly.
terminal *noun*	computer system for punching in food orders	There's one **terminal** in the kitchen and one on the bar.
till *noun*	drawer of a cash register that money is kept in	You need a key to open the **till** and make change.
to go *verb*	to take out of the restaurant	We're just going to order a pizza **to go**.
toppings *noun*	food items that go on top of other food items to add flavour	What type of **toppings** would you like to have on your pizza?
uniform *noun*	clothing that staff members have to wear	The **uniform** here is black pants and a white shirt.
waiter, waitress *noun*	staff member in charge of taking orders and serving food and beverages	When I got promoted from a hostess to a **waitress** I started making tips.
waiting list *noun*	list of groups who want a table to eat at	We have a twenty minute **waiting list** tonight.
warm up *verb*	heat food to an enjoyable temperature for eating	Would you mind **warming up** the baby's bottle for me?
well-done *adjective*	cooked for longer than average	The meat was so **well-done** it had no flavour.
wine list *noun*	a menu of all of the wine you can order from the glass, litre, or bottle	You will notice that we have a lot of local wine on our **wine list**.
winery *noun*	a place where wine is made, tasted, and sold	There is another **winery** up the hill that you might enjoy stopping at.
wine tasting *adjective*	sampling different types of wine	If you are intersted in trying some wines you should go on a **wine tasting** tour.

Chapter 06 Are you ready to order?

Conversation : Are you ready to order?

Waiter : Are you ready to order now?

Guest 1 : Yes. I'll have T-bone steak.

Waiter : How would you like your steak, sir?

Guest 1 : Oh, Well done, please.

Waiter : How about you, ma'am?

Guest 2 : I'll have pork chop.

Waiter : Would you like to have some salad or some soup?

Guest 1 : I want some onion soup.

Guest 2 : I like some fresh salad with thousand island dressing.

Waiter : What would you like to drink, sir?

Guest 1 : I'll have some ice tea. What about you, honey?

Guest 2 : I want lemonade.

Waiter : Would you like anything else, sir?

Guest 1 : No, that's all.

Waiter : I'm going to repeat your order, sir.
Well done T-bone steak, pork chop, salad, onion soup, a glass of ice tea and lemonade. Is that correct, sir?

Guest 1 : Perfect. By the way, how long will it take?

Waiter : It will take about fifteen minutes.

Vocabulary Tips

- order 주문하다
- Well done(medium, rare)

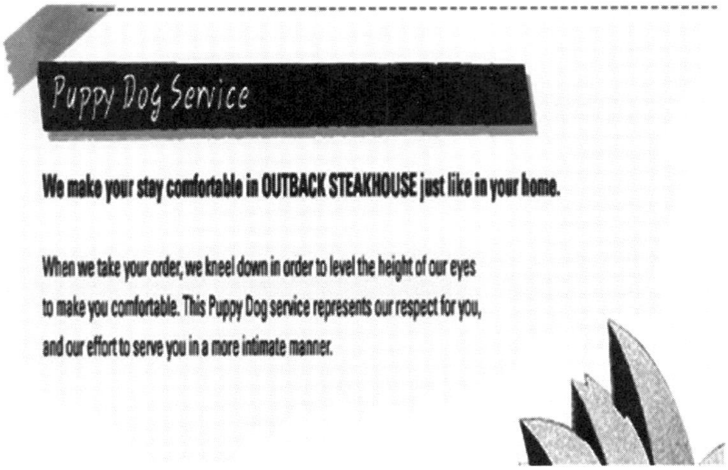

Hotel Terminology

- **Accommodation Capacity :** 숙박 수용력, 고객에게 제공이 가능한 총 숙박시설.
- **Full House :** 모든 객실이 점유되어 100%의 판매율을 나타내는 뜻.
- **Vacancy :** 베이컨시, 객실이 풀 하우스(Full House)가 아닌 상태로 판매 가능 객실이 아직 남아 있음을 의미한다.
- **Tip : To Insure Promptness** 민첩한 서비스를 보장받기 위해 서비스맨에게 베푸는 손님의 호의(봉사료).

Further Study

Vegetables and Fruits for Culinary Art

cucumber	오이	lettuce	상추	spinach	시금치
green beans	강낭콩	leek	부추	pea	완두콩
sesame	깨	mushroom	버섯	celery	샐러리
cabbage	양배추	asparagus	아스파라거스	peach	복숭아
radish	무	prune	서양자두	walnut	호두
red pepper	고추	raisin	건포도	apricot	살구
eggplant	가지	carrot	당근	kiwis	키위
parsley	파슬리	watermelon	수박	pumpkin	호박
Chinese cabbage	배추	bean sprout	콩나물	ginkgo nut	은행
green onion	파	sesame leaves	깻잎	persimmon	감

Reading about Tourism

Risa's letter : She is working as a receptionist for the summer in a hotel in Hongkong

Hello Kate,

How are you? I am enjoying my new job – it's very interesting and varies and I meet lots of people. The hotel is little but everyone here is well-qualified and the standard of service is high. It's a good hotel – they have lots of facilities for children and disabled people. The staff knows lots of languages so I am not learning very much Chinese because everyone speaks to me in per fect English. Hong Kong is a fantastic place. What are you going to do this summer? Do you want to visit me? Then we can explore the city together. Let's stay in touch.

Lisa

Vocabulary Tips

- well-qualified 자격을 갖춘
- facilities 시설
- disabled people 장애인

Did You Know . . .?

How long does it take to fly to Australia? From Europe it'll take anywhere from 20-25 hours. Most flights will have a stopover somewhere in Asia. From Los Angeles there are direct flights to Sydney which take about 15 hours. Flying to New Zealand(Auckland) is about the same, although New Zealand is a little closer to the United States, and a little farther from Europe. 25 hours from London, 20 from New York, and about 12 hours from Los Angeles.

VISUAL ENGLISH : HOSPITALITY INDUSTRY

Write the correct word(from the list below) **to describe each picture:**

(a) hairnet /(b) slice of lemon /(c) salad /(d) spatula /(e) shot glass /(f) pool table /(g) pot /(h) frying pan /
(i) soup /(j) grill

	(　　　　　)		(　　　　　)
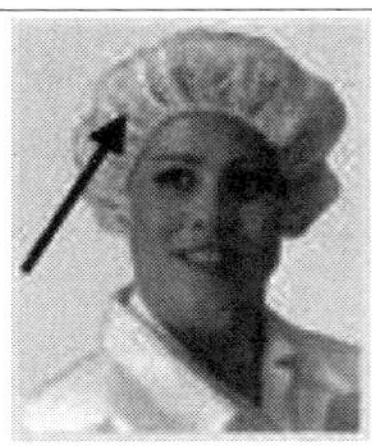	(　　　　　)		(　　　　　)
	(　　　　　)		(　　　　　)
	(　　　　　)		(　　　　　)
	(　　　　　)		(　　　　　)

Exercise – ENGLISH FOR RESTAURANT STAFF/EMPLOYEES

Fill in each blank with the correct word. If both words can be used, choose the one that sounds more natural in each situation:

1. I'm sorry for the ______(tardiness/delay). Your food will be right out.

2. Are you paying together, or would you like separate ______(bills/receipts)?
(=Americans say "checks")

3. There's an automatic 15% ______(grace/gratuity) added to parties of 8 or more.

4. We accept all ______(primary/major) credit cards.

5. The bread is free-of- ______(charging/charge).
(=You don't have to pay for it)

6. The drinks are in the ______(back/rear) of the menu.

7. We have ______(plenty/plentiful) of(=many) vegetarian options as well.

8. Follow me, please - I'll ______(show/seat) you to your table.

9. You can get the salad on the ______(side/separate).
(=not on the same dish as the main meal)

10. It'll ______(take/last) about half an hour to prepare.

The Menu

Understanding the Menu

If you are going to be working in a restaurant, it is important that you understand the menu. Different menus use different words to mean the same thing. They also use certain words to make food sound more delicious. It isn't just the server who should know the menu. Hosts, bartenders, and bussers may also get asked questions about the menu from the guests. Cooks have to know the menu inside-out as well. After all, if an item says it is smothered in mozzerella cheese it can't just have a sprinkling of cheddar.

Most menus are divided into sections. You may need to help a guest find the entrees, or desserts. A guest might call a drink a beverage or a refreshment. Learn the different terms that are used so that you can understand and serve your guests promptly and accurately.

Menu Section

	Also Known As	**Example Items**
Appetizers	Appies, Finger Food, Combo Platters, Snacks, Starters	Garlic Bread, Cheese Plate, Nachos
Salads (and Soups)	Garden Fresh, Greens, Light Fare, Lighter Favourites, Low Calorie Choices, Low-fat Selections	Tossed Salad, Caesar Salad, Soup of the Day
Sandwiches	Burgers, From the Deli, From the Grill, Lunch Menu, Wraps	Grilled Chicken Sandwich, Veggie(Garden) Burger, Steak Sandwich
Italian	Noodles, Pasta, Pizza	Spaghetti, Pepperoni Pizza, Fettucini
Main Course	Entrée, Dinners, Main Dish, Main Event	New York Steak, Chicken Stirfry, Hearty Stew
Sides	Accompaniments, On the Side, Side Dishes	French Fries, Rice, Grilled Veggies
Seafood	Catch of the day, Fish, Fresh from the Sea	Fish and Chips, Battered Shrimp, Smoked Salmon
Mexican	South of the Border, Tex-Mex	Fajitas, Nachos, Enchilladas
Specialties	Signature items, Favorites, Pleasers, 5 Stars	BBQ Ribs, Hot Wings, Chicken Cordon Bleu
Desserts	Sweets, Treats, For the Sweet Tooth	Apple Pie, Mocha Cheesecake, Banana Split
Beverages	Drinks, Non-alcoholic beverages, Refreshments	Soda Pop, Juice, Milk
Wine and Beer	Coolers, Draft, Liquor, Specialty Drinks, Spirits, From the Bar	House Wine, Jug of Beer, Peach Cider
Kids Menu	Juniors, Kids Stuff, Little Tikes, For the Munchkins	Spaghetti and Meatballs, Cheeseburger, Chicken Fingers

Descriptive Words and Expressions on a Menu

Menus often contain special language to make items sound delicious. These words and expressions can also convince the guests to order more food, such as appetizers or dessert. It is useful for servers to learn these expressions in order to sound more knowledgable and achieve better sales. In many English speaking countries, especially North America, having higher sales means earning better tips.

Description	Meaning	Example item
available with	Guests can have this food served a different way.	All burger selections are **available with** whole wheat buns.
bottomless (free refills)	Guests can have more without paying.	Coffee and tea is **bottomless**.
chunky	many large pieces of meat or vegetables	A steaming bowl of **chunky** vegetable soup
coated in, glazed	covered in a sauce(often before cooking)	Breast of chicken **coated in** teriyaki sauce
crispy	makes a crunchy sound when you chew	Caesar salad with fresh lettuce and **crispy** croutons
drizzled with	a small amount of liquid poured over top	Apple pie and vanilla ice cream **drizzled with** butterscotch
finished with	final step of the food preparation	A generous portion of spaghetti and garlic tomato sauce, **finished with** homemade meatballs
fresh	just off the farm/ out of the garden/	All omelettes are made with three **fresh** egg whites.
garnished with	decorated with	Our dinners are **garnished with** fresh parsley and seasonal fruit.
generous portion, heaping, loaded with	a large amount of	All sandwiches are served with a **generous** portion of fresh cut fries.
home style, homemade, made from scratch	from a recipe(not a package)	Try our chef's **homemade** chili with fresh baked bread.
juicy	with liquid remaining for taste	Garden salad with **juicy** tomatoes, cucumbers, and onions

lightly breaded, battered	rolled in bread crumbs, eggs, or other mixture and cooked	Our fish is **lightly battered** in beer.
marinated in	left in fridge to soak up sauce/juice/flavoring	Our steaks are **marinated in** a rich peppercorn sauce.
medley	variety, mixture	A vegetable **medley** tossed in olive oil and served over rice
mouth watering	appearance causes mouth to salivate	Finish your meal off with one of our **mouth watering** desserts.
on a bed of	on top of a layer of	A ginger chicken stir fry served **on a bed of** rice
seasonal	produce varies at different times during the year	Ask your server about our **seasonal** fruit pies.
seasoned with	herbs and spices added	Roasted chicken **seasoned with** fresh basil and oregano

Matching Exercise

Match the menu items with the menu section they belong in.

1	Dessert	a	*Big Daddy's Hamburger with fresh cut fries*
2	Starters	b	*Homemade Iced Tea*
3	Specialties	c	*Junior Spaghetti and Meatballs*
4	Refreshments	d	*Peach pie a la mode*
5	Seafood	e	*Mouth watering garlic cheese toast*
6	Sides	f	*Loaded mashed potatoes*
7	Kids Menu	g	*Chef Brian's homestyle chili*
8	Sandwiches	h	*Lemon and herb glazed Salmon*
9	Spirits	i	*Seasonal tossed greens*
10	Salads	j	*1/2 litre house white*

ANSWERS: 1d, 2e, 3g, 4b, 5h, 6f, 7c, 8a, 9j, 10i

Restaurant Review

레스토랑에 들어서면 웨이터가 smoking seat(흡연석)을 원하는지 non-smoking seat(금연석)을 원하는지 묻는다. 안내를 받아 일단 테이블에 앉게 되면 웨이터가 가져온 메뉴판을 보고 원하는 것을 주문한다(order). 술이나 음료수 같은 drink(마실 것)는 음식과 함께 주문하는 것이 보통이지만 반드시 그럴 필요는 없다.

식사는 appetizer(전체) 요리로 시작하는데, 다음 요리를 즐기기 위해 입맛을 돋우는 것이므로 약간만 먹는 것이 좋다. 한편, seafood(해물)를 주문할 때는 생선의 신선도를 확인해야 한다. 만일 생선이 상한(stale)것 같으면 즉시 웨이터에게 교환해달라고 한다.

생선 요리에는 차가운 white wine(백포도주)이 어울린다. 백포도주는 손의 열기로 더워지지 않게 잔 받침대를 쥐고 마신다.

다음으로는 steak(스테이크)와 같은 육류로 구성된 entree(주요리)가 나온다. 스테이크를 주문할 때는 rare(살짝 구운), medium(중간 정도로 구운), well-done(바싹 구운) 등의 원하는 종류를 명확히 알려줘야 한다. 고기가 부드러우면(tender) 다행이지만 질긴(tough) 경우엔 돈만 버릴 수도 있으니 잘 알아보고 주문한다. 스테이크에는 red wine(적포도주)를 곁들여 마신다. 적포도주는 따뜻하게 마셔야 하므로 잔 몸체를 감싸쥐고 마신다.

Dessert(후식)로는 과자나 젤리, 아이스크림 등이 나온다. 야채나 여러 종류의 치즈가 나오기는 하는데 포크를 사용하여 야채를 치즈에 찍어 먹으면 된다.

레스토랑마다 chef(주방장)의 recipe(요리법)가 다양해서 같은 이름의 음식도 다른 flavor(맛)가 나기 마련이다. 그런데 음식이 맛 있으면(delicious) 다행이지만, 자기 taste(입맛)에 맞지 않을 수도 있으므로 집집마다 specialty(잘 하는 음식)를 알아두는 것이 좋다. 또한 음식을 즐길 줄 아는 gourmet(미식가)는 세계 여러 곳의 cuisine(요리)을 맛보려고 여러 레스토랑을 순례한다. 미식가들은 요리를 주문할 때, ingredient(재료)까지 함께 알려주기도 한다. 그리고 자기가 특히 싱겁거나 짜게 먹는 경우도 미리 알려주면 좋다. 때로는 주방이 아니라 레스토랑 한켠에 있는 정원이나 뜰 같은 patio(파티오)에서 직접 grill(그릴)에 seasoning(양념)을 한 meat(고기)를 구워(roast)먹는 경우도 있다.

Bill(계산서)은 주문 시에 웨이터가 테이블에 놓아 두는데, 그렇지 않은 경우엔 식사를 마친 후에 계산서를 가져오게 하거나 카운터에서 직접 계산한다. 이때 세금을 뺀 음식값의 15~20%를 팁으로 준다. 물론 음식 맛이나 서비스가 좋지 않다면 주지 않아도 된다.

- appetizer 전체, 오르되브르
- bill 계산서(=check, tab)
- chef 주방장
- cuisine 요리 ; the style of cooking which is most characteristic of a country or a district
- delicious 맛 있는

- dessert 디저트, 후식
- drink 음료수, 술
- entree, 주요리(=main course)
- flavor 맛, 풍미
- gourmet 미식가, 식도락가 ; a person who knows a lot about food and cooking and who enjoys eating high-quality food
- grill 그릴 ; 석쇠나 구이용 철판
- ingredient 요리재료 ; a food that is used with other foods in the preparation of a particular dish
- lobster 바닷가재
- meat 고기
- medium(steak) 중간 정도로 구운
- non-smoking seat 금연석
- order 주문하다
- pastry 페이스트리 ; cake, pie, tart 등의 과자류 xxxxxxx
- patio 파티오 ; 옥외 테라스
- rare(steak) 살짝 구운
- recipe 요리법 ; a set of instructions that tell you how to cook something
- red wine 적포도주
- roast 굽다
- seafood 해물
- seasoning 양념, 조미료
- sour 신, 시큼한
- specialty 전문으로 하는 음식 ; a special food that is always very good in a restaurant
- stale 상한
- steak 스테이크
- taste 입맛, 취향
- tender(고기가) 부드러운
- tough(고기가) 질긴
- vegetable 야채
- well-done(steak) 바싹 구운
- white wine 백포도주

Chapter

07 In-flight Meal

Conversation : Excuse me, sir, we are serving dinner now

Flight Attendant : Excuse me, sir, we are serving dinner now.

Passenger : Oh, good. What do you have?

FA : We have Indian style chicken tandoori with nan and Korean style barbecue with rice.

P : I will have the Indian chicken tandoori with nan.

FA : Sure, what would you like to drink, sir?

P : I will have a glass of red wine and a bottle of perrier, please.

FA : I am terribly sorry, sir, we're out of perrier now. But I will get you a glass of red wine. The wine we have tonight is Carmen Reserva from Chile. Will it be okay for you, sir?

P : Certainly, I love Chilean wine. But it's too bad that you're out of perrier. Do you have any other carbonated water?

FA : We have club soda, is it okay for you, sir?

P : Club soda? Well, okay…then, could you please bring me one on the rocks with a slice of lemon, please?

FA : Sure, coming right up, sir.

P : Thank you so much, Miss. Oh! One more thing, I've been having a terrible headache since I got on board. Could you please bring me some Tylenols or Advil?

FA : Sure thing, I'll be right back with you in a second.

P : Thanks a million, you're so kind.

Vocabulary Tips

- flight attendant 승무원(steward, stewardess)
- in-flight meal 기내식 종류(fish, pork, beef)
- carbonated water 탄산수

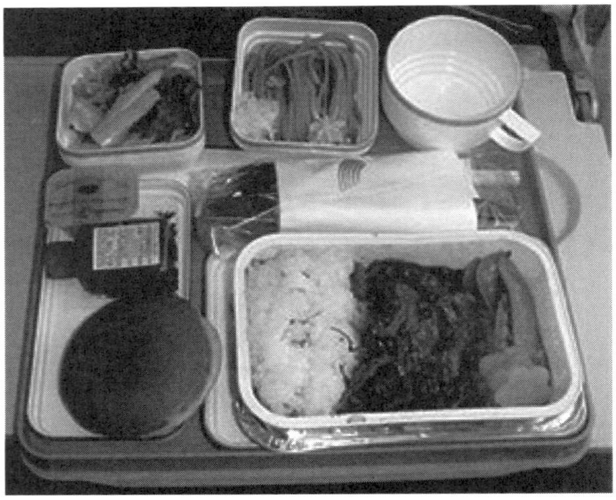

An airline meal or in-flight meal is a meal served to passengers on board a commercial airliner. These meals are prepared by airline catering services. The first kitchens preparing meals in-flight were established by United Airlines in 1936. These meals vary widely in quality and quantity across different airline companies and classes of travel. They range from a simple beverage in short-haul economy class to a seven-course gourmet meal in long-haul first class.

Vocabulary Tips

- on board 탑승한
- catering service 출장연회 서비스(업)
- haul(몸을) 간신히 움직이다,(특정 상황에서 이동하는) 거리[여정/길]

Hotel Terminology

- **Closet :** 옷장으로 안에는, 슬리퍼, 워드로브(Wardrobe), 금고(safe) 등이 있다.
- **Toilet Tissue :** 욕실이나 공중화장실에 고객의 편리를 위해 비치시켜 놓는 화장지로 얼굴 화장지와 구별된다.
- **Pick Up Service :** 호텔과 연결하여 공항으로 손님을 태우고 가는 차편으로 예약 고객의 요청에 의하여 공항 또는 터미널에서 고객을 영접하여 호텔에 체크 인 시키는 서비스를 뜻하며 체크 아웃 시에도 서비스가 가능하다.
- **Complimentary :** 호텔 선전을 위한 목적 등으로 무료로 제공하는 객실 또는 기타 물질적 서비스를 말하며, 보통 약칭하여 Comp(콤프)라고 한다.

Further Study

Read the following check–in procedures. Are they true(T) or false(F)?

F 1 You have to be at the airport thirty minutes before your flight.
2 You must not put your name and address on your baggage.
3 It is not a good idea to have old labels on your baggage.
4 You cannot take any objects on the flight that aren't yours.
5 You can take medicines and expensive objects on board with you.
6 You can take a child's toy gun on the flight with you.
7 You must make copies of your software before you fly.
8 You should look at the destination tag details on your ticket.

Match the words and definitions.

1	departure lounge	a	bags that do not go in the passenger cabin.
2	delay	b	area where passengers wait
3	cabin	c	connected
4	valuables	d	slow down or cause to be late
5	checked baggage	e	security area where you get on the plane
6	attached	f	things that you own that cost a lot of money
7	gate	g	get on a plane, train or boat
8	board	h	area in the plane where the passengers sit

Reading about Tourism

Hospitality Industry

The hospitality industry is one of the fast-growing industries in the world. it offers some exciting careers and a lot of job satisfaction. But it isn't easy to work in a hotel - the peak holiday season is hard work, with employees often working long hours and sometimes seven days a week.

Every staff member, from the housekeeper to the hotel manager, is responsible for the hotel. In small hotels, one manager is usually responsible for rooms, the food and beverage service, registration and general management. There is a wide variety of jobs in large hotel, including administration jobs such as accountant and marketing executive.

Hotel employees get paid sick leave and holidays, as well as other benefits like free food and, occasionally, free holidays! However, the hospitality industry is different from other industries. Hospitality is people dealing with people, from the porter to the hotel manager. If you don't like people, this isn't the career for you.

Vocabulary Tips

- employee 직원
- accountant 회계담당
- marketing executive 마케팅 이사
- sick leave 병가
- benefit 혜택

Airline Announcements : 기내 안내방송

- Listen to some typical public announcements made in an airport or airplane.
  공항이나 비행기에서 들을 수 있는 전형적인 안내방송 입니다.

Pre-boarding Announcement : 탑승 전 안내방송

- Good afternoon passengers.
  승객 여러분 안녕하십니까.
- This is the pre-boarding announcement for flight 89B to Rome.
  이것은 로마행 비행기 89B를 위한 탑승 전 안내방송입니다.
- We are now inviting those passengers with small children, and any passengers requiring special assistance, to begin boarding at this time.
  저희는 지금 이 시간에 탑승을 시작하기 위해 특별한 도움을 필요로 하는 어린아이, 그리고 모든 승객들을 초대합니다. the disabled 장애인, the elderly 노인
- Please have your boarding pass and identification ready.
  탑승권과 신분증을 준비하시기 바랍니다.
- Regular boarding will begin in approximately ten minutes time. Thank you.
  탑승은 약 10분 후에 시작될 것입니다. 감사합니다.

Final Boarding Announcement : 최종 탑승 안내방송

- This is the final boarding call for passengers Erin and Fred Collins booked on flight 372A to Kansas City.
  이것은 캔자스시티 행 비행기 382A를 예약한 에린과 프레드 콜린스 승객을 위한 최종 탑승 안내방송입니다.
- Please proceed to gate 3 immediately.
  즉시 3번 게이트로 향하시길 부탁드립니다.
- The final checks are being completed and the captain will order for the doors of the aircraft to close in approximately five minutes time.
  최종 점검이 완료되고 있으며, 기장은 약 5분 후에 비행기의 문을 닫을 것을 명령 하였습니다.
- I repeat. This is the final boarding call for Erin and Fred Collins. Thank you.
  반복합니다. 에린과 프레드 콜린스를 위한 마지막 탑승 호출입니다. 감사합니다.

Pre-flight Announcement : 비행 전 안내방송

- Ladies and gentlemen, welcome onboard Flight 4B7 with service from Hong Kong to San Francisco.
  신사 숙녀 여러분, 홍콩발 샌프란시스코행 비행기 4B7를 탑승하신 것을 환영합니다.
- We are currently third in line for take-off and are expected to be in the air in approximately seven minutes time.
  저희는 이륙을 위해 현재 세 번째 줄에 있으며, 약 7분 후 비행할 것으로 예상됩니다.

• We ask that you please fasten your seat belts at this time and secure all baggage underneath your seat or in the overhead compartments.
저희는 당신의 좌석 벨트를 지금 즉시 고정하고, 좌석 아래 또는 위 짐칸에 수하물을 넣으시길 부탁드립니다.

• We also ask that your seats and table trays are in the upright position for take-off.
저희는 또한 이륙을 위해 당신의 의자와 테이블 트레이를 똑바로 서게 부탁드립니다.

• Please turn off all personal electronic devices, including laptops and cell phones.
노트북과 휴대폰을 포함한 모든 개인 전자제품을 꺼주시길 부탁드립니다.

• Smoking is prohibited for the duration of the flight.
흡연은 비행하는 동안 금지되어 있습니다.

• Thank you for choosing Mountain Airlines. Enjoy your flight.
마운틴 항공을 선택해 주셔서 감사합니다. 즐거운 비행이 되길 바랍니다.

Captain's Announcement : 기장의 안내방송

• Good afternoon passengers. This is your captain speaking.
승객 여러분 안녕하십니까. 이것은 여러분의 기장의 방송입니다.

• First I'd like to welcome everyone on Rightwing Flight 86A.
첫째로 저는 Rightwing 비행기 86A에 있는 모든 사람들을 환영합니다.

• We are currently cruising at an altitude of 33,000 feet at an airspeed of 400 miles per hour. The time is 1:25 pm.
저희는 현재 시간당 4백마일의 속도로 3,3000피트 고도에서 순항하고 있습니다. 지금 시간은 1시 25분입니다.

• The weather looks good and with the tailwind on our side we are expecting to land in London approximately fifteen minutes ahead of schedule.
날씨가 좋아 보이고 우리측이 순풍이여서 예정된 일정보다 약 15분 정도 먼저 런던에 도착할 것으로 예상됩니다.

• The weather in London is clear and sunny, with a high of 25 degrees for this afternoon.
런던의 날씨는 맑고 해가 떴으며, 오후에는 25도 정도로 올라갈 것입니다.

• If the weather cooperates we should get a great view of the city as we descend. ⇄ ascent
만약 날씨가 허락한다면 내려가면서 저희는 도시의 멋진 전망을 볼 수 있습니다.

• The cabin crew will be coming around in about twenty minutes time to offer you a light snack and beverage, and the inflight movie will begin shortly after that.
약 20분 동안 승무원이 당신 주변에 와서 가벼운 스낵 및 음료와 영화를 제공하는 시간이 곧 시작될 것입니다.

• I'll talk to you again before we reach our destination.
저희의 목적지에 도달하기 전에 다시 얘기 하겠습니다.

• Until then, sit back, relax and enjoy the rest of the flight.
그때까지, 앉아서 편안하고 즐거운 비행의 휴식을 즐길 수 있습니다.

Safety Briefing : 안전 브리핑

- Ladies and gentlemen, on behalf of the crew I ask that you please direct your attention to the monitors above as we review the emergency procedures.
  신사 숙녀 여러분, 승무원을 대신하여 우리의 비상 절차 검토를 위해 모니터에 주의를 기울여 주시기 바랍니다.
- There are six emergency exits on this aircraft.
  이 항공기에는 6개의 비상구가 있습니다.
- Take a minute to locate the exit closest to you.
  당신의 가장 가까운 출구를 찾는 데 몇 분이 걸립니다.
- Note that the nearest exit may be behind you.
  당신의 가장 가까운 출구가 뒤에 있을 수도 있습니다.
- Count the number of rows to this exit.
  출구의 열 번호를 계산합니다.
- Should the cabin experience sudden pressure loss, stay calm and listen for instructions from the cabin crew.
  * should = if
  급격히 압력이 떨어짐을 경험했을 시, 침착하게 승무원의 지시를 듣고 가만히 있어야 합니다.
- Oxygen masks will drop down from above your seat.
  산소 마스크는 당신의 좌석 위에서 아래로 떨어질 것입니다.
- Place the mask over your mouth and nose, like this.
  이와 같이 당신의 입과 코 위에 마스크를 놓습니다.
- Pull the strap to tighten it.
  끈을 조여서 당깁니다.
- If you are traveling with children, make sure that your own mask is on first before helping your children.
  만약 당신이 아이들과 여행 중이라면, 당신의 마스크를 먼저 하기 전에 당신의 아이를 도와주고 확인합니다.
- In the unlikely event of an emergency landing and evacuation, leave your carry-on items behind.
  만약에 비상 착륙과 피난할 경우, 당신의 반입품목을 남겨두고 떠납니다.
- Life rafts are located below your seats and emergency lighting will lead you to your closest exit and slide.
  구명 뗏목은 좌석 아래에 위치하며, 비상조명이 가까운 출구와 슬라이드로 당신을 이끌 것입니다.
- We ask that you make sure that all carry-on luggage is stowed away safely during the flight.
  저희는 당신의 모든 반입 수화물이 비행하는 동안 안전하게 적재되어 있는지 확인 부탁드립니다.
- While we wait for take off, please take a moment to review the safety data card in the seat pocket in front of you.
  우리가 이륙을 기다리는 동안, 당신의 앞주머니에 안전 데이터 카드를 잠시 검토하시길 바랍니다.

Did You Know . . .?

How long does it take to fly to Australia? From Europe it'll take anywhere from 20-25 hours. Most flights will have a stopover somewhere in Asia. From Los Angeles there are direct flights to Sydney which take about 15 hours. Flying to New Zealand(Auckland) is about the same, although New Zealand is a little closer to the United States, and a little farther from Europe. 25 hours from London, 20 from New York, and about 12 hours from Los Angeles.

VISUAL ENGLISH : HOSPITALITY INDUSTRY

Write the correct word(from the list below) to describe each picture:

(a) bathroom /(b) key /(c) towel /(d) curtains /(e) elevator /(f) lobby /(g) pillow /(h) coffeemaker /(i) lamp /(j) bell

	( )		( )
	( )		( )
	( )		( )
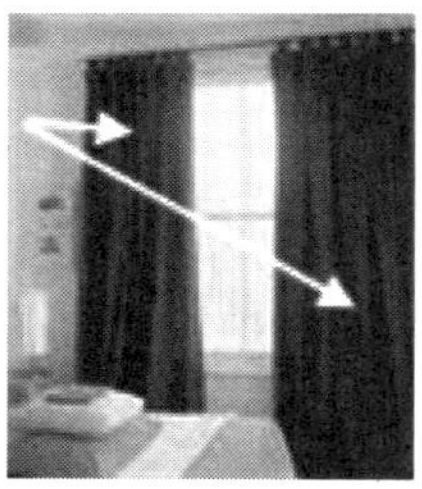	( )		( )
	( )		( )

Exercise – ENGLISH FOR RESTAURANT STAFF/EMPLOYEES

Fill in each blank with the correct word. If both words can be used, choose the one that sounds more natural in each situation:

1. I'm sorry, but our kitchen ______(stops/closes) at 11:00 PM.

2. Would you like anything for ______(sweets/dessert)?

3. How was ______(all/everything)?

4. Our ______(house/home) wine is Concha y Toro from Chile.

5. Would you like to take a look at our wine ______(description/list)?

6. Our ______(special/specialty)(=what we do best) is Tandoor Chicken.

7. We stay open until the last customer ______(leaves/goes).

8. A ______(sampler/diversity) plate gives you a chance to try several different items at once.

9. We're ______(finished/out) of the(NAME OF DISH).
(=We have no more(NAME OF DISH) left.

10. The ______(portions/sizes) are very big.

Behind the Bar

Tending bar requires special skills, such as learning special recipes, measuring, mixing and serving drinks, and chatting with guests. No matter which country you are working in, you are sure to come across English patrons who want a cold drink. Study the lists and expressions bartenders use. Then read the dialogue and check your understanding.

Glassware

brandy snifter	
half litre/litre	a glass container for serving house wine
highball glass	a tall straight glass
martini glass	
mug	a cup or glass with a handle used for hot beverages
pint glass	20 oz glass for draft
pitcher/jug	approximately 60 oz container for draft or water
rock glass/tumbler	short glass for mixed drinks
shot glass	1 oz glass for shots and shooters
sleeve	12 oz glass for draft
wine glass	

Classic Cocktails

There are many different ways to prepare classic cocktails. Every bar or restaurant has rules about how much alcohol to put in a cocktail and how to build it. The following recipes do not contain specific amounts. Use them to learn the names of the cocktails, liquors, and mixes.

Black Russian	vodka, coffee liqueur, on ice(for a white russian-add milk)
Bloody Mary	vodka, tomato juice, tobasco sauce, Worcestershire sauce, salt, pepper, celery salt, slice celery, on ice
Cosmopolitan	vodka, orange liqueur, cranberry juice, lime, on ice
Daquiri	light rum, lime juice, sugar, blended with ice(for a strawberry daquiri use strawberry mix or syrup)
Long Island Iced Tea	vodka, gin, rum, orange liqueur, lemon juice, cola, on ice
Margarita	tequila, lime, salt, blended with ice
Martini	gin, dry vermouth,(garnish with olive)
Pina Colada	rum, coconut milk, pineapple juice, blended with ice
Screwdriver	vodka and orange juice, on ice
Tom Collins	gin, lemon juice, sugar, soda water, on ice

Common Liquor

Gin	clear alcohol flavoured with juniper berries
Liqueur	various sweet alcohols
Rum	clear alcohol made from sugar cane, origin Caribbean
Vodka	clear alcohol made from grain or potato, origin Russia
Whisky(Rye in Canada)	light brown alcohol made from grain, origin Scotland
Tequila	golden or clear alcohol, origin Mexico

Beer and Coolers

Domestic	beer from country that bar is located in
Local	beer brewed nearby
Cans	beer served in a tin
Bottles	beer served in glass bottle
Draft	beer on tap
Keg	beer in a large barrel
Ciders	alcoholic drink from apples or other fruit
Coolers	premixed and bottled alcoholic drinks

Sample Conversation

Bartender: Hi there. What can I get for you?

Guest: I need something cold.

Bartender: You've come to the right place.

Guest: Do you have any specials on?

Bartender: We have highballs on for half price.

Guest: Sorry, I meant for beer.

Bartender: Our beer special tonight is a pitcher of local draft with a half dozen wings for $12.99.

Guest: I guess I should have brought a friend. I think I'll just have a Heineken for now.

Bartender: Sure, would you like that on tap or in a can?

Guest: Do you have it in a bottle?

Bartender: No, I'm afraid we don't.

Guest: That's okay. I'll take a pint.

Bartender: A pint of Heineken coming up.

Guest: Actually, you better just make it a sleeve.

Bartender: Sure. And should I start you a tab?

Guest: No, I'm driving. How much do I owe you?

Bartender: $5.25.

Guest: Here's 6. Keep the change.

Bartender: Thank you.

Airline Review

출국을 위해 공항에 도착하면 domestic line(국내선)이나 international line(국제선=flight)의 boarding area(탑승장)를 찾아가야 한다. 우리나라의 김포공항은 청사 건물들이 따로 있어서 두 곳의 구별이 쉽지만, 외국 공항에는 한 청사 내에 함께 있는 경우가 있으므로 주의해야 한다.

먼저 자신이 이용할 airline(항공사) check-in counter(탑승 창구)로 가서 check-in(탑승수속)을 해야 한다. Airline ticket(항공권)과 passport(여권)를 창구에 제시하면 좌석이 지정된 boarding pass(탑승권)를 발급받게 된다. 이때 window seat(창가 좌석)이나 aisle seat(통로 좌석) 등 원하는 좌석을 말해준다. 다음에는 check-in baggage(탁송하물)로 부치고 claim check(수하물표)를 받는다. 수하물이 제한 무게를 초과하면 excess baggage charge(추가 수하물 운임)를 물어야 하므로 짐의 부피를 줄여서 집을 나서는 것이 현명하다.

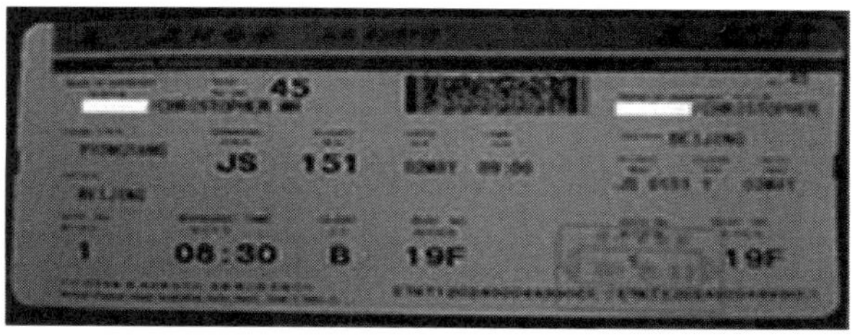

탑승 수속을 마친 뒤에는 customs(세관)를 통과하는데, 이때 귀금속이나 외제품들을 신고해야(declare) 한다. 신고를 안 하면 귀국 시 외국에서 산 물건으로 간주되어 세금을 물게 될 수도 있다. 다음에는 detector(검색대)에서 소지품 검사와 몸 수색을 받는다.

출국 절차의 마지막 단계로 emigration(출국신고)을 하게 된다. 이때는 여권, 탑승권을 제시하고 embarkation card(출국신고서)에 도장을 받아야 한다.

출국 절차의 마치고 탑승권에 적힌 gate(탑승구)로 가면 된다. 시간 여유가 충분할 경우엔 공항 라운지의 duty-free shop(면세점)을 이용할 수 있다.

Destination(목적지)에 도착하게 되면 port of disembarkation(도착지) 공항의 세관에서 immigration(입국심사)을 받게 된다. 소지 물품의 명세를 적은 customs declaration form(여행자 휴대품 신고서)을 여권, visa(비자)와 함께 customs official(세관원)에게 보여주면 purpose of visit(방문목적), duration of stay(체류기간) 등의 질문을 한 뒤 admission(입국허가)을 해준다. 하지만 동물, 식물 등의 특정 소지물이 있을 경우엔 quarantine(검역소)도 거쳐야 한다.

입국 수속을 마치면 baggage claim area(수하물 찾는 곳)에서 자기 짐을 찾고 공항 앞에서 택시나 limousine bus(리무진버스)를 타고 행선지로 간다.

- admission 입국 허가
- airline 항공사
- airline ticket 항공권
- aisle seat 통로 좌석
- baggage 수하물(=luggage)
- baggage claim area 수하물 찾는 곳
- boarding 탑승
- boarding area 탑승장
- boarding pass 탑승권
- carry-on baggage 기내 휴대용 수하물
- check-in 탑승 수속
- check-in baggage 탁송하물
- check-in counter 탑승 창구
- claim area 수하물 찾는 곳
- claim check 수하물표
- customs 세관
- customs declaration form 여행자 휴대품 신고서
- customs official 세관원
- declare 신고하다
- departure 출발(↔arrival)
- destination 목적지
- detector 검색대
- domestic line 국내선
- duration of stay 체류기간
- duty-free shop 면세점
- embarkation card 출국신고서
- excess baggage charge 추가 수하물 운임
- flight 항공편(=airplane)
- gate 탑승구
- immigration 출국신고, 입국심사
- international line 국제선
- limousine bus 리무진 버스
- one-way ticket 편도편
- passport 여권
- port of disembarkation 도착지
- purpose of visit 방문 목적
- quarantine 검역소
- round trip ticket 왕복표(=return ticket)
- visa 비자, 입국사증(=green card)
- window seat 창가 좌석

Chapter 08 Travel

Conversation : I want to travel around Australia.

Travel Agent : Hello. Can I help you?

Customer 1 : Yes. We want to go Australia.

Travel Agent : Australia? OK. Have a seat and we'll see what we can do.

Customer 2 : Thanks. Our daughter is there and we want to go out and do a bit of travelling with her.

Travel Agent : So were you thinking about a package tour, perhaps?

Customer 1 : Well, we were, but the problem is that Mary's already out there. I mean, there's not much point paying an airfare for her.

Customer 2 : We haven't really got a lot of money for this.

Customer 1 : We just want to travel around out there with her, you know.

Travel Agent : So you'd prefer to do things on your own? Be free to move around in your own time?

Customer 1 : Yes!

Travel Agent : You want something not too expensive …

Customer 2 : No,

Travel Agent : … but you want to book your flights and so on before you go?

Customer 1 : Yes, that's right. What do you think? What should we do?

Travel Agent : Well, probably your best option is to travel out to Australia independently, and then once you're there, take a tour run by a local tour operator. Where is your daughter, by the way?

Customer 2 : In Melbourne.

Travel Agent : Ah, that's great. There are many tourist attractions there. And when exactly do you want to travel?

Customer 2 : Well, ideally on the 20th of July. We can't really go any earlier.

Travel Agent : And what about your stay? How long would you want to be away?

Customer 2 : Three weeks, we thought. It would be nice to stay longer, but …

Travel Agent : Three weeks is fine. Now, let's see. Your daughter is in Melbourne, you said?

Customer 1 : Yes, so we thought we'd spend a couple of days there at the beginning while we get used to the time difference.

Travel Agent : Good idea. It's a big difference. It's a bit of a shock for the body clock. So, let's see … it's Mr. and Mrs. …?

Customer 2 : Brown.

Travel Agent : And have you booked with us before, by any chance?

Customer 2 : We haven't actually. We were passing and …

Travel Agent : That's no problem, Mrs. Brown. It was just to see if we had you on the computer. Now, what have we got that might interest you …

Vocabulary Tips

- Have a seat = Sit down, Be seated
- airfare 항공료(bus fare, taxi fare = rates)
- tourist attractions 관광명소

Hotel Terminology

- **Inventory :** 재고조사, 판매전표와 출고전표 취급을 확실히 하고 재료 원가율에 유의하여 적정원가율을 항상 유지하도록 한다. 일일 재고조사(Daily Inventory)와 월 재고조사(Monthly Inventory) 등이 있다.
- **Airtel :** 미국에서 공항 근처에 지어진 호텔을 에어텔이라고 부를 때가 있다. 그러나 이것은 일반적인 용어가 아니고, 에어포트 호텔(Airport Hotel)과 같은 뜻으로 보통 사용되고 있다.
- **Do Not Disturb :** 호텔의 객실에서 종업원이나 손님의 출입을 제한하는 표시로서 손님이 문에 걸어두는 표지에 쓰는 문구이다.
- **Walk-in Guest :** 예약 없이 들어오는 고객
- **In-Bound :** 국내로 들어오는 외국 관광객 ↔ Out-Bound 국외로 나가는 국내 관광객

Further Study

A travel agent deals with many inquiries like the following.

total price of the holiday / dates of the flights / names of the people travelling / types of accommodation / method of payment / destination / car rental

A travel agency is a private retailer or public service that provides tourism related services to the public on behalf of suppliers such as airlines, car rentals, cruise lines, hotels, railways, and package tours. In addition to dealing with ordinary tourists most travel agencies have a separate department devoted to making travel arrangements for business travelers and some travel agencies specialize in commercial and business travel only. There are also travel agencies that serve as general sales agents for foreign travel companies, allowing them to have offices in countries other than where their headquarters are located.

Vocabulary Tips

- retailer 소매업자, 소매상; 소매업
- on behalf of ~을 대신[대표]하여
- headquarters 본사

◎ **You are the tour operator. Use the information in the box to answer to your travellers.**

Tour feature	Tour : Beaches of Cebu(Philippines)
Tour area + Type	Beach resort holiday
Air fares	Not included. Client must organize
Transfers	Transfers to and from airport on first and last day included. Private minibus used
Meals	Breakfast & evening meal. Breakfast & lunch on day of departure
Hotels	All hotels locally owned and managed. Maximum size = 24 rooms. All hotels have private gardens and luxury-class service, etc.
Groups(=7+people)	Not accepted. Maximum 4 people per booking. No minimum
Discount for groups	None
Travel agent's commission	10%
Brochures	Available next month for next season

Reading about Tourism

Careers Questionnaire

What are your working style? Look at the questionnaire and tick(√) the qualities and skills which describe you. And which three skills are most important for a career in tourism?.

Questionnaire					
QUALITIES					
I am					
smart	□	extrovert	□	hardworking	□
flexible	□	organized	□	practical	□
creative	□	friendly	□	confident	□
scruffy	□	shy	□	nervous	□
SKILLS					
I enjoy meeting new people.					□
I enjoy working as part of a team.					□
I like working independently.					□
I am good at explaining things.					□
I am good at dealing with people.					□
I can make people relax.					□
I like working under pressure.					□
I know how to use computers and technology.					□
I can do more than one thing at the same time.					□
I feel confident about dealing with money.					□
I am willing to work long hours.					□
I am good at languages.					□

Did You Know . . .?

The five busiest airports in Asia(in terms of international passengers) are: 1) Hong Kong International Airport, 2) Singapore Changi Airport, 3) Narita International Airport, 4) Dubai International Airport, and 5) Suvarnabhumi Airport(Bangkok, Thailand).

The five busiest airports in Europe(in terms of international passengers) are: 1) London Heathrow Airport, 2) Charles de Gaulle International Airport(Paris, France), 3) Amsterdam Airport Schiphol, 4) Frankfurt Airport, and 5) London Gatwick Airport.

The five busiest airports in North America(total passenger traffic, both domestic and international) are: 1) Hartsfield-Jackson Atlanta International Airport, 2) O'Hare International Airport(Chicago), 3) Los Angeles International Airport, 4) Dallas-Fort Worth International Airport, and 5) Denver International Airport.

VISUAL ENGLISH : HOSPITALITY INDUSTRY

Write the correct word(from the list below) **to describe each picture:**

(a) remote control /(b) reception desk(=front desk) /(c) minibar /(d) pool /(e) safe /(f) staircase /(g) uniform /
(h) credit card /(i) luggage /(j) jacuzzi

	(　　　　)	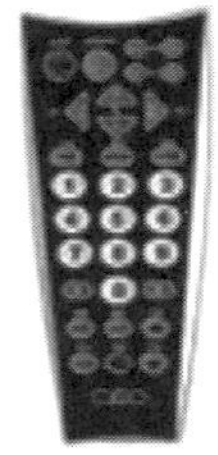	(　　　　)
	(　　　　)		(　　　　)
	(　　　　)		(　　　　)
	(　　　　)		(　　　　)
	(　　　　)		(　　　　)

Exercise – ENGLISH FOR TRAVEL AGENTS

Fill in each blank with the correct word. If both words can be used, choose the one that sounds more natural in each situation:

1. There are no seats available for the date that you _____(requested/recalled).

2. How _____(flexible/changeable) are you?(= How much are you willing/able to change your schedule?

3. Would you be _____(interesting/interested) in renting a car while you're there?

4. We've got some great _____(deals/dealings) on airplane tickets to Dubai right now.

5. That flight is _____(full/complete). Let's try to find you a seat on another flight.

6. The _____(layover/takeover)(= time you have to wait for your connecting flight) in Paris is two hours.

7. We can _____(arrange/make)(= organize) your entire trip.

8. Will you be traveling _____(alone/lonely)?

9. I booked you a flight on October 1st, _____(returning/coming) on October 15th.

10. You also qualify for a 10% senior _____(discount/deal).(= 10% reduction in price for older people)

English for Tour Guides

Being a tour guide is a very important job. In many cases, the tour guide is a traveller's first impression of a foreign country. In other cases a tour guide may be responsible for teaching tourists about the culture and sites in a city or town. In addition, many tour guides hold the responsibility of teaching tourists about safety. Even if you are only responsible for taking a tourist from the airport to his or her hotel, it is your responsibility to make the short trip interesting, informative, and safe. The following pages will help you learn some important vocabulary and phrases that you can use with your English-speaking tourists. Check your understanding as you go.

Vocabulary(nouns)

Word	Meaning	Example sentence
activities	things to do	There are lots of **activities** that the whole family will enjoy.
architecture	design of a building	The **architecture** of this building is typical of the Renaissance age.
art gallery	place to look at professional paintings and drawings	We are going to visit the **art gallery** where local painters exhibit their art.
attractions	places for tourists to see	The water park is our most recent **attraction**.
bearings	feeling for understanding one's location/surroundings in an unknown area	If you're having trouble getting your **bearings** just remember that the mountains are west.
business district	area in a city that has many offices	Keep in mind that this is the **business district** so that grocery store may be expensive.
castle	a building for royalty	No one has lived in this **castle** since the last king died twenty years ago.
church	a place to worship God	The **church** is the central meeting place in this town.
conveniences	things that make life easier	There you will find all of your **conveniences**, from suntan lotion to shampoo.
custom	something people of a region do often	It's a **custom** to hang beads in the windows at this time of year.
en route	on the way	While we are **en route** to the hotel I will point out the beach and the golf course.
entertainment district	a place where there are theatres and concert halls	If you want to catch a movie while you're here, the **entertainment district** is off to your left.
exception	something/someone that does not follow the usual rules or expectations	With the **exception** of Johnson Street, it is safe to walk around here at night.

exhibition	objects(i.e. art) displayed for a short time for the public to view	It may be tough to find parking with the car **exhibition** on this week.
grocery store/ supermarket	place to buy food to take home	Since you have a kitchenette at your hotel you will need to know where the **grocery store** is.
highlight	the best part	People often say that the **highlight** of their trip is the botanical gardens.
legend	a person or story known for a long time	According to an old **legend**, a sea monster lives in this lake.
lobby	front entrance	We will meet in the **lobby** at 8 am sharp.
locals	people who live in an area	The **locals** are usually happy to show tourists around.
location	place where something can be found	This **location** is the best because you don't need to bother renting a car.
map	shows roads and directions to places	I'll give you each a **map** so you can follow along as we walk.
market	place to buy fresh food and homemade items	Every Sunday there is a farmer's **market** on Wade Street.
monument	a statue/structure that honours an event or person	This **monument** honours the men and women who died during the war.
museum	a place where historical items are displayed	The **museum** charges a small fee for adults, but children are free.
necessities	things that people need for every day living	We recommend that you only carry **necessities** in your purse and leave everything else at the hotel.
original state	the way something appeared from the beginning	Except for the roof, this home has been left in its **original state**.
photograph	picture taken with a camera	You may not take **photographs** here, but you can purchase a postcard.
postcard	a card with a picture on one side(usually an object or place that tourists see) that can be mailed without an envelope	The gift shop has many great souvenirs, such as **postcards** of the beautiful waterfalls.
questions or concerns	things that tourists may want to say or ask	The plane almost missed the **runway** because it was such a bad storm.
request	something that has been asked for politely	The driver has made a **request** that you throw all of your garbage in the bin at the front on your way out.
restaurant district	part of a town/city with many places to eat	You will see there are many more eateries to choose from when we head to the **restaurant district**.

ritual	tradition, custom, action(religious or cultural) that people do often	It is an old native **ritual** to dance during the sunrise.
scenery	natural beauty to look at	It is impossible to capture the beauty of this **scenery** in pictures.
settlers	people who first made a home in an area	The original **settlers** relied on oxen to carry their wares.
shopping district	area of town where there are many stores	You may want to save some spending money because we'll be visiting the **shopping district** this afternoon.
site	place,location	This is the **site** of a very famous battle.
stairway/stairwell	steps going up or down	The **stairwell** is very steep, so please watch your step.
street people	people who live on the street, often begging for money	You may be surprised how many **street people** ask you for money.
surroundings	things that you see around you	I hope you enjoy the castle and its **surroundings**, including the secret garden.
voice	the sound you make when speaking	I apologize for my **voice** today as I have a bit of a cold.
voucher	a piece of paper that shows you have paid	Don't forget to bring your **voucher** for a free coffee in the hotel lobby.
waterfront	piece of land next to an ocean, lake, or river	There will be plenty of live entertainment down at the **waterfront**.
window	glass that you look out	We can peer in the **window** but I think they are probably closed for the day.

Vocabulary(verbs)

Word	Meaning	Example sentence
arrive	reach a destination	I am glad to see you all **arrived** safely.
close	to finish	We **will close** the tour with a view of the city at sunset.
continue on	keep going	If you're all finished looking here, we will **continue on** with the tour.
depart	leave	The last ferry **departs** at 4pm, so make sure you don't miss it.
enjoy	have a good experience	I have **enjoyed** meeting all of you today.
expect	think that something will be/happen a certain way	You probably weren't **expecting** to see snow.
permit	allow	You are **permitted** to have a beverage on the bus, but please do not eat any food.

proceed	go forward	Please **proceed** all the way to the back of the bus.
raise (a hand)	lift	If you have any questions during the tour, please **raise** your hand.
recommend	suggest	We **recommend** that you only keep a small amount of cash in your wallet.
refer	suggest	I will gladly **refer** you to my favourite restaurants, if you are interested.
relax	sit back and enjoy time in peace	Tomorrow you will have a day to just **relax** on the beach.
show someone around	take people to see an area	When we get to the museum someone else will **show** us around.
sit back	relax in a seated position	Please **sit back** and enjoy the bus tour.
speak up	talk louder	If you need me to **speak up** or slow down, please let me know.

Vocabulary(adjectives)

Word	Meaning	Example sentence
ancient	very old	The **ancient** village has been left untouched.
beautiful/gorgeous	very nice looking	You will find **beautiful** homemade jewellery in that shop.
breathtaking	when a view is very impressive	Under the starlight the waterfall is simply **breathtaking**.
customary	traditional	It is **customary** to shake hands and bow as you enter.
dangerous	not safe	It is **dangerous** to accept a ride from a local.
devastating	very sad, unfortunate	The tsunami was **devastating** for local hotels.
elegant	attractive, yet simple	There is an **elegant** dining room for guests to eat in.
enormous	very large	This **enormous** sculpture stands one-hundred feet high.
exciting	makes one feel very happy/energetic	It's so **exciting** to see new places, isn't it?
extensive	covers a lot	This house has an **extensive** history, and you can read more in the brochures.
fascinating	very interesting to learn about/see	It is **fascinating** to know how people lived back then.

haunted	believed to have ghosts living there	The house is said to be **haunted** and no one has lived in it for fifty years or more.
heritage	of historical importance	The government named this school as a **heritage** site last year.
international	around the world	Every year it is an **international** celebration, with people coming from as far away as Africa.
lovely	very nice(appearance or personality)	This is a **lovely** place to sit and watch the local birds.
magnificent	amazing	This part of town is known for its **magnificent** wall murals.
popular	liked by many	June is the most **popular** time for tourists to come here.
prevalent	very noticeable	Crime is **prevalent** in the old parts of town.
reconstructed	built again	The village was **reconstructed** after the major fire in 1910.
restored	returned to its original state	All of the antique furniture has been professionally **restored**.
safe	not dangerous	The water is **safe** to drink here.
scenic	nice to look at(nature)	We will go up to the balcony for a **scenic** view of the grounds.
superb	very good(i.e. service, food, entertainment)	The children put on a **superb** concert at Christmas time.
thrilling	exciting	Cliff jumping is a **thrilling** experience for those of you who aren't afraid of heights.
unbelievable	too amazing/strange to seem true	It is **unbelievable** what some of these street entertainers can do.
visible	able to be seen	The top of the tower may not be **visible** because of the fog.

Boarding Review

항공기 boarding(탑승)은 business class(비즈니스석) 승객들이 먼저 탑승하고, 다음에는 economy class(일반석) 승객들이 탑승하게 된다.

기내에 탑승하면 flight attendant(기내 승무원)의 안내에 따라 항공원에 기재된 좌석을 찾아 앉는다. 휴대한 짐은 aisle(통로)에 놓지 말고 머리 위쪽에 있는 overhead rack/compartment(짐 넣는 선반)이나 앞좌석 밑에 넣어둔다.

탑승이 완료되면 cockpit(조종실)의 captain(기장)이 ETA(도착 예정시간)와 stopover/layover(중간 기착지) 등에 대한 안내방송을 한다. 이러한 안내와 함께 승무원들이 life vest(구명조끼) 입는 법을 포함한 비상 시 행동요령 등을 알려준다.

이제 runway(활주로)에서 비행기가 이륙하고(take off) 여행이 시작된다.

기내에서는 승무원들이 다양한 complimentary service(무료 서비스)를 이용할 수 있다. 음악을 듣거나 영화를 볼 수 있고 비치된 각종 신문과 잡지도 읽을 수 있다. In-flight magazine(기내지)에는 in-flight meal(기내식)과 beverage(음료)도 제공된다.

기내의 lavatory(화장실)을 이용할 대는 먼저 화장실 앞 전광판에 occupied(사용 중)라는 표시에 불이 들어와 있는지 확인해야 한다. 요즘은 대부분의 항공사가 모든 좌석을 nonsmoking section(금연구역)으로 지정하고 있고 화장실에서도 흡연을 못 하게 한다. 만일 화장실에서 흡연을 하면 경고음이 울리니까 유의할 것.

출발지의 시각과 도착지의 시각에 차이가 큰 경우에는 jet lag(시차 피로)를 겪게 되므로 장거리 여행 시엔 시차를 잘 계산해서 비행 도중 충분한 수면을 취해야 한다.

그리고 중간 기착지를 경유해서(via) 여행할 때는 connection/connecting flight(접속항공편)으로 갈아타게 되는데, 이때 transit card(재탑승 카드)를 갈아타는 공항에서 발급받아서 재탑승 시 제시해야 한다.

긴 여행이 끝나고 착륙할(land) 시간이 되면 기장의 안내방송을 듣게 된다. 승무원의 안내에 따라 좌석 벨트를 매고(fasten safety belt) 착륙을 기다린다. 도착을 알리는 안내방송이 있은 뒤 기내에서 작성해둔 disembarkation card(입국신고서)와 여권을 가지고 비행기에서 내리면(deplane) 된다.

- aisle(좌석 사이의) 통로
- beverage 음료 ; a drink of any type
- business class 비즈니스석
- captain 기장
- cockpit 조종실(석) ; the small enclosed space where the pilot sits in an aircraft(Ex. He climbed into the cockpit of the fighter)
- complimentary service 무료 서비스
- connection 접속편 비행기(Ex. If the flight is late, we'll miss our connection)
- deplane 비행기에서 내리다.
- disembarkation card 입국신고서
- economy class 일반석
- ETA 도착 예정 시각(=estimated time of arrival)
- flight attendant 기내 승무원
- in-flight feature 기내 영화
- fasten(벨트를) 매다.
- in-flight magazine 기내지
- in-flight meal 기내식
- jet lag 항공 여행에서 시차 때문에 오는 피로
- land 착륙하다
- life vest 구명조끼(=life jacket)
- nonsmoking section 금연구역
- occupied(화장실 등을) 사용 중인(↔vacant)
- overhead rack(기내의 짐 넣는) 선반
- lavatory 화장실
- runway 활주로
- stopover 중간 기착(지)
- take off 이륙하다
- transit card 비행기를 갈아탈 대 제시하기 위해 공항에서 받는 카드
- via ~을 경유하여 ; by way of(Ex. The flight goes via Seattle.)

Chapter
09 Car Rental

Conversation : I'd like to hire a car.

Car Rental Clerk : Hello, Alamo Car Rental. How can I help you?

Renter : Hello, I'd like to rent a car.

Car Rental Clerk : Which model do you want?

Renter : I want a compact car.

Car Rental Clerk : Automatic or manual?

Renter : Automatic, please.

Car Rental Clerk : How long will you be renting it?

Renter : For three days. How much does it cost a day?

Car Rental Clerk : It's 100 dollars for a compact car and 150 dollars for a medium sized car.

Renter : I'd like to hire Sonata, a compact car. How about the insurance?

Car Rental Clerk : You will have to pay 130 dollars including insurance and tax. When you return the car, are you going to fill up the tank or do you want us to do it at 2 dollars per gallon?

Renter : OK, I'll fill'er up. I will pick up the car tomorrow morning at 9 am.

Car Rental Clerk : Great, see you at nine and thanks for calling! Have a nice day.

Renter : You, too.

Vocabulary Tips

- 자동 변속기(automatic), 수동 변속기(manual)
- 자동차 렌탈 보험 CDLW(Collision Damage and Loss Waiver Insurance)

Hotel Terminology

- **Make Up :** 객실청소(예) Make Up Room : 청소가 완료된 방
- **Occupancy Rate :** 호텔 객실 또는 항공기 좌석 이용률
- **Over Booking :** 초과예약, 즉 만원임에도 불구하고 취소가 있을 것을 생각하고 그 이상의 예약을 접수하거나 판매하는 것
- **Over Charge :** 객실 사용기간 초과요금, 즉 체크아웃 시간을 기준으로 하여 일정시간을 초과함에 따라 적용되는 요금. 대개 2시간 이내는 무료. 그 이후부터는 6시까지 Over Charge로서 Half-Day Charge(반값)를 적용하는 것이 보통이다. : late-checkout

Further Study

Vocabulary test of Car Rental : Match the phrases with their definition

1	seven-day rental	a	place where you collect the car
2	air conditioning	b	car hire for one week only
3	collision damage waiver(CDW)	c	in-car temperature control
4	an additional charge	d	insurance cover for the driver
5	third-party liability	e	an extra cost
6	a pick-up location	f	insurance cover for other road users

Transportation in the U.S.

Airplane		
	United Airline Northwest Airline	미국은 Los Angeles와 New York 간 시차가 3시간이나 날 정도로 넓기 때문에 장거리를 자동차로 이동하는 것이 쉽지 않아서 국내선 비행기의 노선이 발달되어 있다.

Train		
	AMTRAK (Express Train)	암트랙. 정식 명칭은 국립철도여객회사(National Railroad Passenger Corporation)이며 연방의 지원을 받아 미국 내 거의 모든 도시 간에 여객열차를 운영하는 철도회사이다.
	Monorail	주로 Chicago(시카고)의 전철에서 볼 수 있는 궤도가 하나뿐인 형태의 전차이다. 시카고에서는 'Loop' 라고 불리우며 운행되고 있다.
	CABLE CAR (Street Car)	지하철이나 버스 이외의 특수한 교통수단으로서 San Francisco와 New Orleans에서 운영되고 있는 케이블 카이다.
	SUBWAY	미국의 대도시 중에서 지하철이나 전차가 발달해 있는 곳은 New York City, Chicago, Washington D.C., Boston, San Francisco 등이며, 이러한 대도시 이외의 지역에서는 찾아보기 어렵다.
Taxi		
	Yellow Cab	주로 뉴욕의 맨하탄 지역에서 운영되며 일반 택시는 그냥 cab 혹은 taxi라고 하면 된다. 택시는 서비스업으로 간주되어, 운임료 이외에 기사에게 팁(tip)을 지불해야 한다.

Car		
	Rent-A-Car	면허증이 반드시 있어야 하지만 차를 빌릴 수 있는 연령제한은 주마다 조금씩 차이가 있으며 신용카드를 제시해야하는 경우가 많다. 차를 빌리면서 사전에 반환장소를 지정할 수도 있다.
	Car	미국에서 가장 일반적인 서민들의 이동수단은 역시 자동차(승용차)이다. 식구들이 여럿인 경우 2, 3대의 자동차를 갖는 것도 보통이다.
	Truck / Van	일반 가정에서도 취향에 따라 트럭이나 (미니)밴을 사용하는 경우도 많으며 짐을 싣고 여행을 하는 경우 유용한 면이 있다.
	RV (Recreational Vehicle)	Motor Home이라고도 불리며 차안에 침실, 부엌, 욕실 등 일체의 필요한 시설이 되어 있는 여가용 '집차'를 말한다. 약간 다른 형태로 자동차에 연결시켜서 끌고 다니는 Camper 혹은 Trailer라는 형태도 있다.
Bus		
	GREYHOUND BUS (Express Bus)	Amtrak과 마찬가지로 미국 내의 거의 모든 주요 도시 간에 고속버스를 연결하는 버스회사이다. 장거리 여행을 위한 버스이므로 버스 뒤편에 화장실이 준비되어 있으며 많은 배낭여행객들이 주로 이용하는 교통수단이기도 하다.
	BUS (City Bus)	우리나라처럼 매우 상세한 노선까지는 운행되지 않지만 지하철이 정비되어 있는 대도시를 제외하면 그래도 시내버스가 중요한 대중교통 수단이다. 우리나라와 다른 점은 운전사가 잔돈을 거슬러주지 않고 교환기도 없다는 점이다.

Reading about Tourism

Car rental USA

- Cheap Car Rental's USA rates include unlimited mileage, breakdown cover, third party insurance, collision damage waiver, taxes & fees.
- Car hire collection points at all major airports in USA
- No additional fee to pickup from premium locations such as airports in USA.
- One way rentals available.
- Low cancellation/amendment charges.
- Rates with or without GPS.
- Quick immediate quotes.
- No credit card charges.

Did You Know . . .?

Europe has over 60 low-cost airlines, the biggest of which are Easyjet, Ryanair, and Germanwings. These airlines fly to destinations around Europe, and sometimes sell tickets for as low as 1 € each way. The drawbacks of flying a low-cost airline is that once you're on the plane you have to pay for pretty much everything. Some airlines even require you to pay for every bag that you check or bring with you.

VISUAL ENGLISH : HOSPITALITY INDUSTRY

Write the correct word(from the list) to describe each picture:

(a) TV /(b) microwave / c) cot /(d) bed /(e) 'do-not-disturb' sign /(f) alarm clock /(g) armchair /(h) phone book /(i) plastic cups /(j) hallway

	( )		( )
	( )		( )
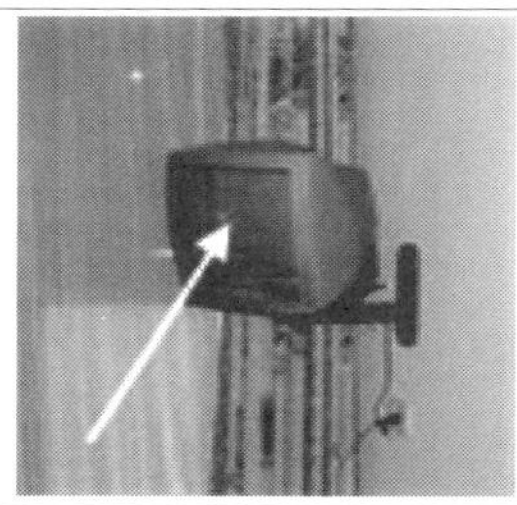	( )		( )
	( )		( )
	( )		( )

Exercise – ENGLISH FOR TRAVEL AGENTS

Fill in each blank with the correct word. If both words can be used, choose the one that sounds more natural in each situation:

1. Will this be a one-way ticket, or a _____(returning/return) ticket?(= in the United States, "round-trip ticket" is used)

2. I've heard nothing but _____(positive/benefits) things about this resort.

3. Are you interested in buying travel _____(insurance/assurance)?

4. This is probably your best _____(option/optional).

5. We have a lot of _____(package/box) deals(= deals which include air, hotel, and sometimes food/drinks) to Cuba and the Dominican Republic right now.

6. You can _____(upgrade/increase) to a four-star hotel for $200 more.

7. You'll have to _____(confirm/conform) your reservation by the end of tomorrow.

8. The ticket has to be _____(purchased/presented)(= bought) by Thursday.

9. To pay in _____(full/complete) = To pay the entire/whole price

10. A passenger's "_____"(itinerary/journey) is their proposed route of travel(travel plan).

Car Review

미국은 New York 등 일부 대도시를 제외하고는 버스나 metro(지하철) 같은 대중교통이 취약하고 cab(택시)은 fare(요금)가 비싼 편이다. 그리고 집 근처에 슈퍼마켓이 있는 경우가 드물어서 장을 보려고 해도 차를 타고 나가야 한다. 이러다 보니 자동차는 미국인의 필수적이 생활도구이다.

휴일에 driveway(진입로)에 차를 내놓고 세차를 하는 모습은 흔한 풍경이다. 그들은 flat tire(빵구)를 비롯한 간단한 breakdown(고장)의 경우 repair shop(정비소)으로 가지 않고 직접 수리를 한다.

관광객이나 출장 중인 사람들은 rent-a-car(렌터카)를 많이 이용한다. 대부분의 렌터카는 secondhand(중고)이지만 저렴한 가격에 이용할 수 있다. 종류는 세피아 크기의 compact car(소형차)에서부터 롤스로이스 같은 luxury car(고급차)에 이르기까지 다양하며, jeep(지프) 같은 off-road vehicle(비포장 도로용 차량)과 유개 트럭인 van(밴)도 임대할 수 있다. 임대료는 대개 날짜로 계산해서 30~40달러 정도이지만 mileage(주행거리)로 계산하는 경우도 있다. 차량 절도가 많으므로 렌터카의 license number(차량번호)를 반드시 적어두어야 한다.

만일 운전 중에 이상이 있으면 즉시 차를 노변에 대고(pull over) hood(후드)를 열어 계기들을 점검해야 한다. 출근 시에 driveway에서 후진하거나(back) 고속도로를 달리다가 collision(충돌)으로 차의 한 쪽이 움푹 들어가는(dent) 사고도 자주 생긴다. 사고가 나면 즉시 차를 견인하도록(tow) 해서 정비소에서 mechanic(정비사)의 정비를 받아야 한다.

미국의 많은 도로가 직선으로 곧게 뻗어 있기 때문에 교외에서의 장거리 주행 시에는 transmission(변속기)을 고정시키고 accelerator(가속페달)와 brake(브레이크)만 사용해서 운전이 가능하다.

미국인들의 운전 문화에서 배울 점은 특별한 경우를 제외하고는 horn(경적)을 울리지 않는 다는 것이다. 즉 불필요한 소음으로 타인에게 피해를 주지 않으려는 배려인 듯 싶다.

- accelerator 가속 페달
- back 후진하다 = rear
- brake 브레이크
- breakdown 고장
- cab 택시(=taxi)
- collision 충돌(=crash)
- compact car 소형차
- dent 부딪혀서 움푹 들어간 곳(Ex. Somebody made a large dent in the back of my car while it was parked.)
- driveway(도로에서 차고로 들어오는) 진입로
- fare 요금
- flat(tire) 빵구가 난
- garage 차고
- hood 후드, 보닛
- horn 경적
- jeep 지프
- license number 차량번호
- license plate 차량 번호판
- luxury car 고급차
- mechanic 정비사
- metro 지하철(Ex. Shall we take the metro, or go by bus?)
- mileage 주행거리
- off-road vehicle 비포장 도로용 차량
- pull over(차를) 길가에 대다(Ex. The policeman signalled to him to pull over.)
- rent-a-car 렌터카
- repair shop 정비소
- secondhand 중고의(=used)
- tow 견인하다 ; to pull a disabled car along behind a vehicle
- transmission 변속기
- van 밴 ; a medium-sized vehicle with windows all round, used for carrying more people than an ordinary car
- vehicle 차량 ; a machine such as a bus, car or van that carries people or things

Chapter 10

Business or Pleasure?

Conversation : Can I see your passport?

Immigration Officer: Can I see your passport and boarding pass, please?

Traveller: Here they are.

Immigration Officer: Where are you from?

Traveller: I'm from Korea.

Immigration Officer: What's the purpose of your visit? Business or pleasure?

Traveller: Travel.

Immigration Officer: Is this your first visit to the U.K?

Traveller: Yes, it is.

Immigration Officer: How long are you going to stay in the U.K?

Traveller: About two weeks.

Immigration Officer: Where are you going to stay?

Traveller: The Ritz Carton in London.

Immigration Officer: What's the address?

Traveller: I don't know the address.

Immigration Officer: How much money do you have?

Traveller: Some cash. I have a credit card.

Immigration Officer: Do you have anything to declare?

Traveller: No, I have nothing to declare.

Immigration Officer: Is this all you have?

Traveller: Yes, it is.

Immigration Officer: Thank you. Enjoy your stay.

Traveller: Thanks.

Vocabulary Tips

- Immigration Officer 출입국 관리관

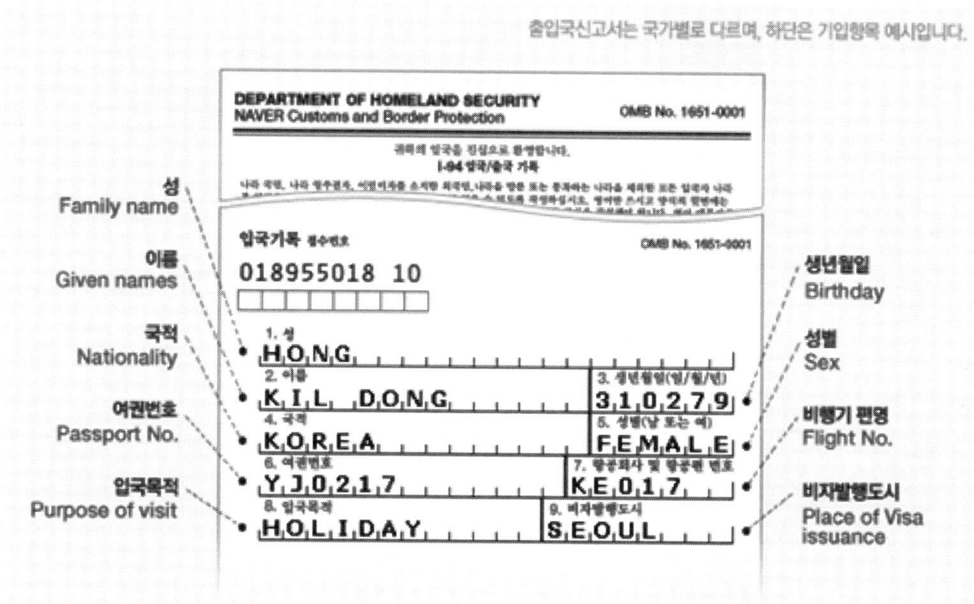

An arrival card is a legal document used by a country's immigration authorities to provide passenger identification and a record of a person's entry to a country. [1] It also provides information on health and character requirements for non-citizens entering a particular country. [2] Some countries like the United States and Singapore attach this card to a departure card where the latter is retained in the

alien's passport until his eventual departure. The arrival card can also be combined with items found in a customs declaration card which some countries require incoming passengers to fill-out separately.

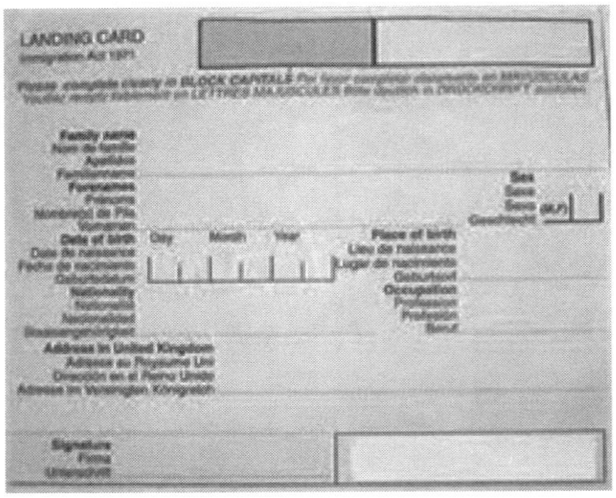

An arrival card may also be known as an incoming passenger card, landing card and disembarkation card.

Information on the card itself. The information requested varies by country. Typically the information requested on the departure card includes:

- Full name
- Nationality
- Date of Birth
- Passport number, place of issuance and expiration date
- Flight number or name of aircraft, ship or vehicle
- Purpose of trip: vacation, education/study, visiting relatives/families, business, diplomatic
- Duration of stay
- Destination (next stop of disembarkation)
- Address in country

A visa (from the Latin character visa, lit. "paper that has been seen")[1] is a document showing that a person is authorized to enter the territory for which it was issued, subject to permission of an immigration official at the time of actual entry.

A passport is a document, issued by a national government, which certifies the identity and nationality of its holder for the purpose of international travel. The elements of identity are name, date of birth, sex, and place of birth.

Customs Declaration : Information on items being brought into the country which may be of interest to customs and quarantine authorities. Travelers are generally required to sign, date, and declare the information is true, correct, and complete.

Hotel Terminology

- **ETA**(Estimated Time of Arrival) **:** 도착 예정시간
- **ETD**(Estimated Time of Departure) **:** 출발 예정시간
- **Duty Free Shop :** 출국 내국인이나 외국인을 위한 면세물품 판매점
- **Bus Boy :** 식당에서 고객의 식사가 끝난 후 식탁을 치우는 등 버스와 같이 기물과 식사만 운반한다고 하여 붙여진 이름. 웨이터를 보조하는 호텔 종사원으로 Commisde rang(코미 드 랭)이라고도 한다.

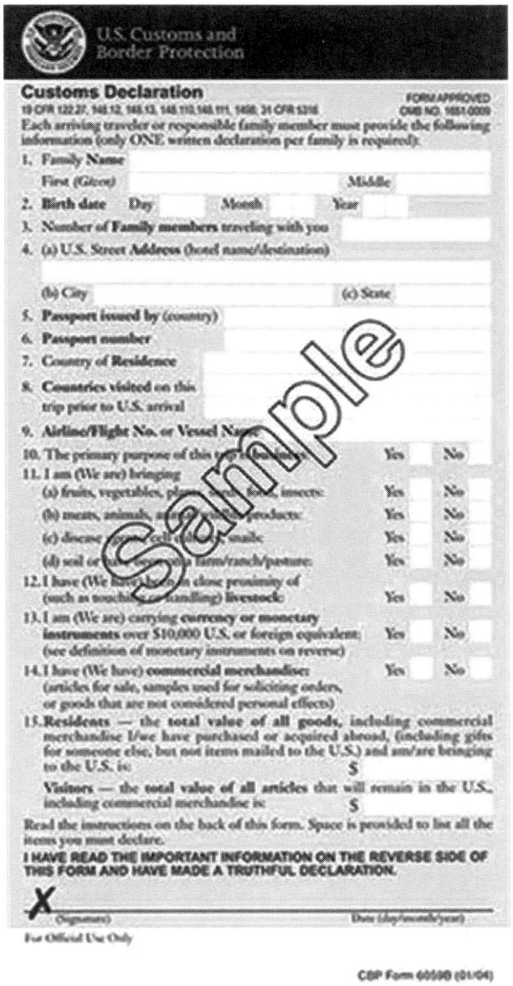
U.S. Customs and Border Protection

Customs Declaration

FORM APPROVED
OMB NO. 1651-0009

19 CFR 122.27, 148.12, 148.13, 148.110, 148.111, 1498; 31 CFR 5316

Each arriving traveler or responsible family member must provide the following information (only ONE written declaration per family is required):

1. Family Name
   First (Given) Middle
2. Birth date Day Month Year
3. Number of Family members traveling with you
4. (a) U.S. Street Address (hotel name/destination)
   (b) City (c) State
5. Passport issued by (country)
6. Passport number
7. Country of Residence
8. Countries visited on this trip prior to U.S. arrival
9. Airline/Flight No. or Vessel Name
10. The primary purpose of this trip is business: Yes No
11. I am (We are) bringing
    (a) fruits, vegetables, plants, seeds, food, insects: Yes No
    (b) meats, animals, animal/wildlife products: Yes No
    (c) disease agents, cell cultures, snails: Yes No
    (d) soil or have been on a farm/ranch/pasture: Yes No
12. I have (We have) been in close proximity of (such as touching or handling) livestock: Yes No
13. I am (We are) carrying currency or monetary instruments over $10,000 U.S. or foreign equivalent: Yes No
    (see definition of monetary instruments on reverse)
14. I have (We have) commercial merchandise: Yes No
    (articles for sale, samples used for soliciting orders, or goods that are not considered personal effects)
15. Residents — the total value of all goods, including commercial merchandise I/we have purchased or acquired abroad, (including gifts for someone else, but not items mailed to the U.S.) and am/are bringing to the U.S. is: $
    Visitors — the total value of all articles that will remain in the U.S., including commercial merchandise is: $

Read the instructions on the back of this form. Space is provided to list all the items you must declare.

I HAVE READ THE IMPORTANT INFORMATION ON THE REVERSE SIDE OF THIS FORM AND HAVE MADE A TRUTHFUL DECLARATION.

X (Signature) Date (day/month/year)

For Official Use Only

CBP Form 6059B (01/04)

Further Study

Complete the questions with the words in the list 1~14.

1	sharp objects	a	Can I have your _____ and _____?
2	ticket	b	Has the flight _____ yet?
3	help	c	Did you pack your _____ yourself?
4	board	d	Are you _____ someone?
5	meeting point	e	What is the _____ of your visit?
6	window	f	Are you carrying any _____ in your hand luggage?
7	aisle	g	Could you _____ me?
8	suitcase	h	Can I _____ you?
9	purpose	i	Has your _____ been in your possession at all times?
10	baggage	j	Are there any _____ seats available?
11	passport	k	Can you tell me where the _____ is?
12	help	l	Is it too late to _____ the plane?
13	checking in	m	Are you _____ any bags today?
14	landed	n	Would you like an _____ seat?
15	meeting		

Reading about Tourism

영어면접 시 자주 나오는 질문

- Tell me about yourself?(자기소개를 해주십시오.)
- What's your strength or weakness?(당신의 강점과 약점은 무엇입니까?)
- What's your favorite hobby?(당신이 좋아하는 취미는 무엇입니까?)
- How do you spend your free time?(여가시간은 어떻게 보내나요?)
- Why did you leave the last company?(이전 회사는 왜 그만 뒀나요?)
- Why should we hire you?(왜 우리가 당신을 뽑아야 하는지 설명해 주세요?)
- Why did you apply to our company? Why do you want to work for this company?(왜 우리 회사를 지원하셨습니까?)
- Please tell me about your part-time job or present company.(파트타임이나 현재 근무하는 회사에 대해 말씀해 주십시오.)
- What kinds of position would you like to have for this company?(우리 회사에서 어떤 일을 맡고 싶습니까?)
- How does the previous experience relate to this position?(이전 회사의 경험이 이번 직무와 어떻게 연관이 되나요?)
- What do you know about this company?(우리 회사에서 대해 아는 것을 설명해 주세요?)
- How do you feel about working overtime?(연장근무에 대해서 어떻게 생각하세요?)
- What is the biggest accomplishment in your life?(인생에서 가장 큰 성취는 어떤 것인가요?)
- What is your expected salary? How much salary do you want to get?(보수는 어느 정도 받길 원하십니까?)
- What's the most important things in your life?(인생에서 가증 중요한 것은 무엇이라고 생각하십니까?)
- What has been the most difficult moment in your life?(인생에서 가장 힘들었던 순간은 무엇이었나요?)
- What's your future plan?(미래 계획은 무엇입니까?)

Did You Know . . .?

In the United States, low-cost airlines such as Southwest and Jetblue are actually known for having better working conditions(and consequently happier employees) than the major American airline companies.

Out of all the airlines in the world, the five best ones(for passengers) are in Asia: Asiana Airlines, Singapore Airlines, Malaysia Airlines, Qatar Airways, and Cathay Pacific.

VISUAL ENGLISH : HOSPITALITY INDUSTRY

Write the correct word(from the list below) **to describe each picture:**

(a) horseback riding /(b) conference room /(c) balcony /(d) beach chairs /(e) phone /(f) bellhop /(g) golf course /(h) chair /(i) cart /(j) sheets

	( )		( )
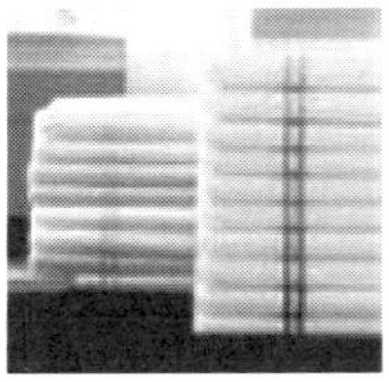	( )		( )
	( )		( )
	( )		( )
	( )		( )

Exercise – ENGLISH FOR FLIGHT ATTENDANTS

This exercise is for flight attendants(stewardesses, stewards, cabin crew, etc.) who want to improve their English in order to communicate better with passengers. It will teach you many useful English terms/expressions used before, during, and after a flight:

overhead / sickness / landing / around / remain / turbulence / tables / fold / flight / serving

1. Make sure your bags are stored in the _____ compartment.(= the compartment above where the passengers sit)

2. Since this a short flight, we'll only be _____ a light snack.

3. We'll be coming _____ shortly to offer you drinks.

4. Sir, please _____ in your seat until the plane comes to a complete stop.

5. If you start to feel nauseous, there are air-_____ bags in the seat pocket in front of you.

6. We're experiencing light _____. There's nothing to worry about.

7. Our in-_____ movie is "The Departed".

8. We'll be _____ in 20 minutes.

9. The little fold-down tables where passengers eat their meals are called "meal trays" or "tray _____."

10. Passengers should _____ up their meal trays prior to(= before) landing.

Airline Vocabulary

Word *part of speech*	Meaning	Example sentence
airfare *noun*	cost of a plane ticket	The cost of your meal is covered in your **air-fare**.
aisle *noun*	the long empty space that you walk down	Please keep your bags out of the **aisle** so that nobody trips.
aisle seat *noun*	the seat that is next to the aisle	I'll give you an **aisle seat** in case you need to walk around with the baby.
assist *verb*	help	Please wait until everyone is off the plane so that we can **assist** you.
baggage *noun*	the bags and suitcases that travellers put their belongings in	I'm afraid your **baggage** got on the wrong airplane.
baggage, luggage claim *noun*	place where you pick up your baggage after arrival	The announcement will direct you to the correct **baggage claim**.
blanket *noun*	warm covering	If you feel cold I can get you a **blanket**.
boarding pass *noun*	part of the ticket that you give to the crew as you step onto the plane	Your must present your **boarding pass** at the gate.
bumpy, rough *adj*	up and down movement of the aircraft	It might be a **bumpy** ride because we are flying through a storm.
cabin *noun*	interior of the aircraft	There is no smoking allowed inside the **cab-in**.
call light *noun*	a button passengers can press to get a crew member's attention	If you need anything, just press the **call light**.
captain *noun*	the person who is in charge of the plane	Would the kids like to go and meet the **cap-tain**?
charter *noun*	discount airline	If you take a **charter** it will cost you half as much.
cockpit *noun*	the part of the plane where the captain and his co-pilots sit	We aren't doing any more tours of the **cock-pit** because it's almost time to land.
comfortable *adjective*	feel good physically, able to relax	Because you have long legs you might be more **comfortable** in an aisle seat.
complimentary *adjective*	free of charge	We offer **complimentary** coffee or tea, but you have to pay for alcohol.
co-pilot *noun*	person who helps the captain fly the plane	If the captain gets sick the **co-pilot** can take over.
domestic *adjective*	within the same country	You should be at the airport two hours ahead of time for **domestic** flights.

emergency exit *noun*	section of the plane that opens in the case of an accident	Are you comfortable sitting next to the **emergency exit**?
e-ticket *noun*	airfare purchased on the internet	You will need to present your identification along with your **e-ticket**.
excess baggage *noun*	heavier/more bags than you are allowed	You can either pay for your **excess baggage** or leave one of your bags behind.
first-class *noun/adj*	more expensive seating, with better services	When you sit in **first-class** you get a better meal to eat.
gate *noun*	place where passengers go to wait to board a plane	**Gate** 3B is down this hall and to your right.
headset, earphones *noun*	device that allows passengers to listen to music or a movie	We will be coming around to sell **headsets** for five dollars.
international *adj*	worldwide	For **international** departures, go up one level.
jet lag *noun*	tiredness due to travelling through different time zones	I'm used to travelling now. My body doesn't suffer from **jet lag** anymore.
land *verb*	returning to the ground after being in the air	We will be **landing** in Tokyo in approximately ten minutes.
life vest, life jacket *noun*	a blow-up device that you put on in an emergency over water	Please take a moment to locate the **life vest** under your seat.
motion sickness *noun*	a bad feeling in the stomach that passengers get during a rough ride	There is a paper bag in front of you in case you experience **motion sickness**.
overbooked *adj*	more passengers than available seats	The flight is **overbooked**. Four of our passengers will have to wait for the next flight.
overhead bin /compartment *noun*	place above the seats for storing luggage	You'll have to put your bag under your seat because all of the **overhead bins** are full.
over-sized baggage *adj*	items that do not fit in suitcases	Infant car seats and sporting equipment can be picked up at the **over-sized baggage** counter.
oxygen mask *noun*	a device that goes over a person's face, provides air in case of cabin air pressure loss	Put your **oxygen mask** on first before putting one on your child.
passport *noun*	document that proves a person's identification and nationality	Please have your **passport** out when you go through security.
pilot *noun*	the person who drives the plane	The **pilot** is circling over the airport until it is safe to land.
refreshments *noun*	drinks and snacks	It's a short flight, so we will be serving **refreshments** but not a meal.

row *noun*	a number of seats beside each other	You are in seat B of **row** nine.
runway *noun*	the strip of land that an airplane takes-off and lands on	The plane almost missed the **runway** because it was such a bad storm.
seatbelt *noun*	device that holds passengers in their seats	Please remain in your seats while the **seatbelt** light is on.
steward(male), stewardess(female), flight attendant, air host *noun*	man or woman who provides service for passengers during a flight	Ask one of the **stewardesses** for a pillow if you're tired.
stopover *noun*	touching down at more than one airport during a flight	It's not a direct flight. We're making one **stopover** in Toronto.
take off *noun/verb*	when the plane leaves the ground	We are next in line to **take off** on this runway.
taxi in, out *verb*	driving an airplane to the correct place for taking off or deboarding	Please remain in your seats until we **taxi in** to the gate.
touch down *verb, noun*	when the aircraft wheels land on the ground	That was a very smooth **touch down**.
turbulence *noun*	rough flight	This **turbulence** should only last a few minutes.
wheelchair *noun*	a seat for pushing elderly, disabled, or injured people	A steward will take you to the gate with a **wheelchair**.
window seat *noun*	seat next to the window where passengers can look out	If your child wants a **window seat** I can move you back a row.

Chapter

11 Where to, sir?

Conversation : Where to, sir?

Driver : Hello, Where to, sir?

Passenger : New York Palace Hotel, please.

Driver : Where are you from?

Passenger : I am from Korea.

Driver : Is this your first time to visit USA?

Passenger : Yes, could you recommend the places where the foreigners visit the most?

Driver : I want to recommend the Cathedral of Saint John Divine.

Passenger : Is that the biggest cathedral in USA? Any other nice places to visit?

Driver : Um, Statue of Liberty, Colombia University, Whitney Museum, etc. How long will you be staying in New York?

Passenger : One week. Is it difficult to visit all of them for one week?

Driver : I guess that it's enough time to tour. In my opinion, at first, you need to go to Colombia University and then go to the Cathedral of Saint John Divine.

Passenger : I won't visit Colombia University. After visiting the Cathedral of Saint John Divine. What places are good to visit?

Driver : Well, Whitney Museum and Lincoln Center will be fine. It is a good choice.

Passenger : Lincoln Center?

Driver : Yes, Lincoln Center is a composite arts center. Especially, the Ballet Building is beautiful at night.

Passenger : Lincoln Center. I'll go there.

Driver : We arrived at your destination. It's 34 dollars.

Passenger: Thank you for introducing me to tourist attractions. Here, keep the change.

Driver : Thank you. Have a nice trip. Good night.

Vocabulary Tips

- Where to, sir? 어디로 모실까요?
- recommend 추천하다
- Statue of Liberty 자유여신상

Hotel Terminology

- **Rooming List :** 단체고객이 도착하기 전에 단체고객의 인적사항을 기록한 투숙고객의 명단이며, 단체객의 사전 등록과 사전 객실 배정을 위해 필요하다.
- **Late Arrival :** 예약시간보다 늦게 도착한 고객
- **Lost & Found :** 고객 분실물 습득 및 신고센터

Further Study

Reasons for travel : Match the words in A with the definitions in B.

A		B	
1	Sightseeing	a	A long hard walk lasting several daysor weeks, usually in the mountains
2	Trade fair	b	Tour or excursion that leaves in the morning and return the same evening
3	Study tour	c	Visiting the famous places in a city or town
4	Trek	d	Trip, often to a city or countryside hotel, that includes Saturday and Sunday
5	Conference	e	Religious or artistic celebration that comes at the same time every year
6	Wedding	f	Large official meeting, often lasting several days, for members of an organization or company to discuss subjects related to their work
7	Pilgrimage	g	Large exhibition and meeting for advertising and selling a project
8	Day trip	h	Visit organized by an airline or tourist resort, etc. where tour operators and journalists can get to know the facilities and services offered
9	Festival	i	Trip to a country or an area that includes visits, lectures, and classes
10	Weekend break	j	Journey or holiday given to a worker or group of workers as a reward for good work
11	Familiarization (or farm) trip	k	Travel to an important religious place
12	Incentive tour	l	Ceremony where two people get married

Vocabulary test : Match these eight adjectives and eight nouns to form more word combinations.

1	cheap	a	memories
2	cultural	b	bars
3	delicious	c	beaches
4	happy	d	heritage
5	relaxing	e	nightlife
6	exciting	f	flights
7	lively	e	break
8	crowded	f	food

Reading about Tourism

London Taxi

Taxis have been a part of London for 300 years. The first ones started in 1662, and were simple horse-drawn carriages. Today, the black London taxi is perhaps the most famous taxi in the world. Its design has changed little in more than 40 years.

It isn't easy to become a London taxi driver. You have to learn a lot about the roads and places of interest - this is called The Knowledge. The Blue Book is a guide that has 400 routes and all the places people may want to go. All applicants must memorize this. When they are ready, applicants take a written exam, and then there more tests. After that, they have to learn an additional 100 main routes from the suburbs into London. Finally, they become licensed and can start taking passengers. The whole process takes one to two years of full-time study!

Currently, there are over 17,000 licensed taxi drivers working in London. If you have a good memory and want to learn more about London, would you like to join them!

Did You Know . . .?

These days it's easier than ever to request a special meal. Whether you're a vegetarian, a vegan, or require a kosher or halal meal, chances are the major airlines will provide you with the proper meal. The good thing about getting a special meal is that you get served first :)

LEARN ENGLISH THROUGH PICTURES – Travel/tourism

Write the correct word(from the list below) **to describe each picture:**

(a) horse and carriage /(b) park /(c) river /(d) prohibited /(f) castle /(g) pub or bar /(h) suitcase /(i) backpack /
(j) gate /(k) pedestrian street

	(　　　　　)		(　　　　　)
	(　　　　　)		(　　　　　)
	(　　　　　)		(　　　　　)
	(　　　　　)		(　　　　　)
	(　　　　　)		(　　　　　)

Exercise – ENGLISH FOR FLIGHT ATTENDANTS

This exercise is for flight attendants(stewardesses, stewards, cabin crew, etc.) who want to improve their English in order to communicate better with passengers. It will teach you many useful English terms/expressions used before, during, and after a flight. Fill in each blank with the proper(best) response from the list below:

charge / stow / duration / request / blanket / fastened / wireless / lavatories / service / items

1. We're going to begin our meal _____ shortly.

2. Please let one of the flight attendants know if you're interested in purchasing(= buying) any of our duty-free _____.

3. All of the _____ are currently occupied.

4. Make sure your seat belt is _____.

5. Passengers are reminded to turn off all cellphones(= mobile phones) and other _____ devices.

6. Are your feet cold? I'll get you an extra _____.

7. Did you _____(= order/ask for) a special meal?

8. The headphones are provided free-of-_____.(= you don't have to pay for them)

9. Your phone has to be turned off for the _____ of the flight.(= for the whole flight)

10. To put your belongings in the overhead compartment = To _____ your belongings in the overhead compartment

Chapter 12

Shopping

Conversation : Cash or charge?

Sales Clerk : Hello, welcome to AK duty free shop. May I help you?
Customer: Can you recommend some handbags?
Sales Clerk : This bag is a good product.
Customer: Oh, it's cute. Do you have anything else?
Sales Clerk : How about this brand? This one is very popular among young generation. Furthermore, it is on sale.
Customer: Good. The design is simple and it is light. It is my style. How much is it?
Sales Clerk : Seven hundred dollars.
Customer: Oh. it's reasonable. I will take it.
Sales Clerk : OK. Cash or charge?
Customer : I will pay by credit card.
Sales Clerk : Do you have any membership card?
Customer : Yes. I have. Can you give me any discounts?
Sales Clerk : Five percent discount, ma'am.
Customer : That is good.
Sales Clerk : Hang on a second. I will wrap it.

Vocabulary Tips

I'm looking for the cosmetics section. 발
* Duty Free Shop : Lotte, Shilla, Donghwa, AK, Paradise, 한국관광공사, JDC

Hotel Terminology

- **Shift :** 근무 조 또는 근무시간을 나타내는 것으로 Night Shift라고 할 때는 야간 근무조를 뜻한다.
- **Mail Service, Courier :** 우편물 서비스, 호텔의 우편물을 집배하거나 발송하는 서비스.
- **Rubber Mat** : 욕조 안에 목욕 시 미끄러지지 않게 까는 것.
- **Bathrug :** 세면 및 세면대를 이용 시에 바닥에 까는 것으로 재질은 면으로 되어 타올 형태와 같게 한다.

Further Study

Air Travel Vocabulary

captain	기장	attendant call	승무원 호출
jetlag	시차	reading light	독서등
altitude	고도	channel selector	채널 검색
occupied	사용중	in-flight magazine	기내 잡지
vacant	비어 있는	in-flight entertainment	기내 영화 등
local time	현지시간	volume control	음량조절
airsick bag	오물봉지	life jacket(vest)	구명조끼
oxygen mask	산소마스크	seat adjustment	좌석조절 버튼
lavatory	화장실	reclining button	좌석조절 버튼
toilet flush	수세핸들	compartment	기내 수화물놓 는 곳
toilet paper	화장지	air/car/sea sick	멀미

flight crew/cabin crew/cabin attendant/flight attendant/steward/stewardess 승무원

Shopping Signs

OPEN	영업중	CLOSED	휴점
OPEN 24 HOURS		ALWAYS OPEN	연중무휴
STORE OPEN 10 A.M.	10시 개점	CLOSED FOR REPAIRS	수리중 휴업
FOR SALE	팔 것	NOT FOR SALE	비매품
SOLD	팔렸음	SOLD OUT	매진
HAND OFF	손대지 말 것	HANDLE WITH CARE	취급주의
PRICE LIST/TAG	정가표	RECEIPT	영수증
PLEASE PAY CASHIER	출납원에게 지불하시오	NO EXCHANGE OR REFUND	교환, 반품 사절
CHANGE	거스름돈	RESERVED	예약마감

Shops and Merchandise

bakery shop	제과점	drug store	약국
gift shop	선물가게	sporting goods	스포츠 용품
flower shop	꽃가게	grocery store	식료품 가게
hardware store	철물점	laundry	세탁소
convenience store	편의점	liquor store	주류 판매점
gas(filling) station	주유소	shopping mall	백화점
men's clothing	남성복	women's clothing	여성복
underwear(lingerie)	속옷	accessories	장신구
electric appliances	전기제품	electronics	전자제품
vegetables	청과물	jewelry	귀금속
tobacco	담배	furniture	가구
apparel	의류	cosmetics	화장품
sports and outdoors	야외활동	wallet, purse	지갑

Reading

샘플 영문 자기소개서 및 이력서 작성 실례

LETTEROFSELFINTRODUCTION

Min-Hyun Kang
48-1 Daelim 2-Dong, Kuro-Gu
Seoul 120-193, Korea
(02)838-2134, 010-xxx-xxxx

Thank you for giving me a chance to introduce myself. My name is Min-Hyun Kang. I am 20 years old. I graduated from Kimp College majoring in English and Tourism. I live in Seoul. There are four in my family. My Dad, my Mom, my Sister and me. I was brought up with care and affection by my family. My father is diligent, my mother is always kind and my elder sister has a strong sense of responsibility. It helped me to gain confidence and independence in my life. I am out-going, creative and hard-working.

The major reason for majoring in English and Tourism is that I want to work in hospitality industry like hotel, duty free shop, travel agency, and airliner. When I took the major, I studied many subjects about service industry such as Marketing, Restaurant Management, Hotel Management and so on. The most interesting subject to me was English for hospitality industry, which encouraged me to take some more subjects about it. I am good with managing personal computers of Internet, Power Point, Excel and Word Process.

During my university life, I tried to travel around the world in order to know the cultures of many countries and make foreign friends. This helped me better understand various cultures and life styles of other counties.

The enclosed resume elaborates on the details of my skills and experience. I'd appreciate the chance to meet with you to discuss how I could be a vital part of your company. You may reach me at the above telephone number or e-mail address. Thank you for your consideration. I look forward to talking with you.

Sincerely,
Daniel Patel

RESUME(Curriculum Vitae)

Rachel Choi

- Address : 104-907, Hanyang Apt, Jung-dong, Mapo-gu, Seoul, 121-871, South Korea
- Home: 82-2-376-4543
- Mobile: 82-10-3456-4356
- D.O.B: August 26, 1993
- Sex: Female
- Email: rachelchoi@naver.com

Objective

- To build my career and work experience in the field of marketing, international sales while having an active interpersonal relationship with associates.

- To achieve global mindset by experiencing international business

- To promote the ability to apply the theoretical and practical knowledge learned in college to hands-on business situations

Experiences

-November.2009 ~December 2010:Paris Baguette(Bakery)

Part-time for sale

■ Products sales and managing a store.

- November. 2010: G20 Seoul Summit 2010

English-Korean translation team leader

■ Translation for foreigner at the event hall.

■ Conducting a tour with foreign tourists.

■ Promote the event to the public.

- February ~ July 2011: PR department in Hanguk University

Internship

■ Documenting school promotional materials.

■ Managing university souvenir for promotion.

-August. 201 : 'Specialty Foods' Trade Mission

English-Korean Translation

■ Translation between Korean buyers and USA food seller.

-June. 2011 ~ Present: International Abilympics(Ability + Olympic) in Seoul

Online Honorary Ambassador

■ Promotion of Olympic posting poster online.

■ Improving awareness for the disabled through education.

-July. 2011 ~ Present: Graduate school of TESOL in Hanguk University

Internship

■ Documenting a TESOL program to promote to elementary, middle school teachers.

■ Devising marketing strategies to make a TESOL program to be activated in the current educational system.

Education

- March.2010 ~ present: Hanguk University, Seoul, Korea

1st Major: English Language & Literature / 2nd Major: Business Administration

Courses completed: Translation, English Phonology, English in the era of Globalization, English and Intercultural Communication, French, Principles of Marketing, International Marketing, Strategic Management, Financial Accounting Principles.

Achievements

- March ~ December. 2009: UNSA(United Nations Students Association of the Republic of Korea), Seoul, Korea

■ Holding a regular general assembly to enhance ideology and objective of UN.

■ Discussing the current UN activities.

■ Promoting interactions among students all over the world.

- March. 2010 ~ February. 2011: Leadership Group '2Wins' in Hanguk

■ As a president of PR department of Leadership Group '2Wins' which helps every student in school to get a quality job, advertising our group's working and holding special lecture in terms of employment.

Skills

- Language - Fluency in both written and spoken English.(TOEFL 81, TOEIC 865, TOEIC speaking Level 7)
- Software - MS Office(expert SPECIALIST with Word, Excel, Power Point)

Volunteer Activities

- International Abilympics(Ability + Olympic) in Seoul

■ Translation volunteering activities for foreigners at the event hall

Reference

Available upon request

Did You Know . . .?

During a recent(2007) survey of low-cost airlines, the Australian company Jetstar won named the "best low-cost airline in the world". In Europe, the honors went to Air Berlin, and in the United States, to Jetblue.

LEARN ENGLISH THROUGH PICTURES

Write the correct word(from the list below) to describe each picture:

(a) path /(b) zoo /(c) train /(d) amusement park /(e) seats /(f) sunset /(g) airplane /(h) tram /(i) flight attendant /(j) souvenirs

	( )		( )
	( )		( )
	( )		( )
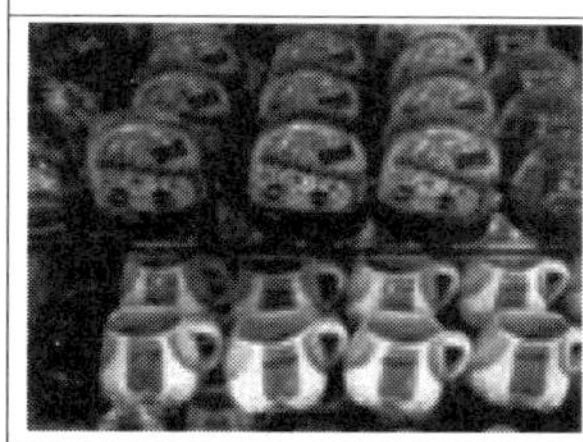	( )		( )
	( )		( )

LEARN ENGLISH THROUGH PICTURES

Write the correct word(from the list below) **to describe each picture:**

(a) cabin /(b) brochure /(c) skis /(d) tickets /(e) bathroom /(f) snowboard /(g) church /(h) money /(i) bus /
(j) bicycle

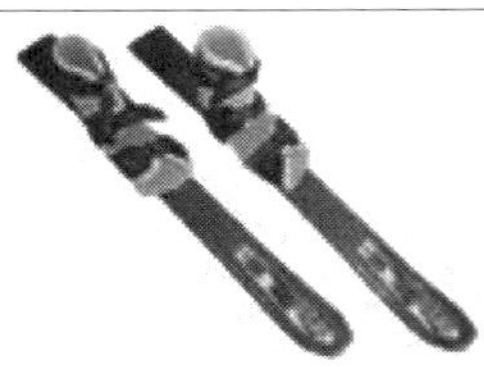	(　　　　)	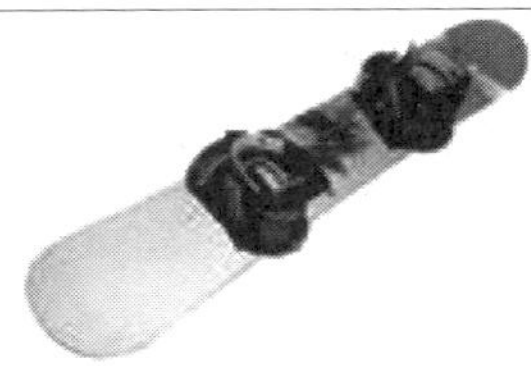	(　　　　)
	(　　　　)		(　　　　)
	(　　　　)	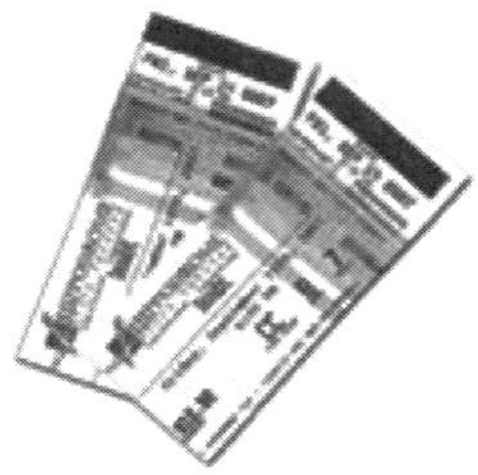	(　　　　)
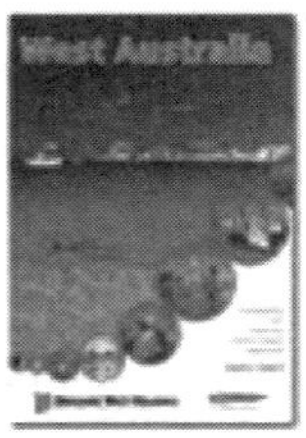	(　　　　)		(　　　　)
	(　　　　)		(　　　　)

LEARN ENGLISH THROUGH PICTURES

Write the correct word(from the list below) **to describe each picture:**

(a) bridge /(b) camera /(c) stadium /(d) motorcycle /(e) fountain /(f) mosque /(g) statue /(h) cemetery /
(i) waterfall /(j) train station

<table>
<tr><td></td><td>(　　　)</td><td></td><td>(　　　)</td></tr>
<tr><td></td><td>(　　　)</td><td></td><td>(　　　)</td></tr>
<tr><td></td><td>(　　　)</td><td></td><td>(　　　)</td></tr>
<tr><td></td><td>(　　　)</td><td></td><td>(　　　)</td></tr>
<tr><td></td><td>(　　　)</td><td></td><td>(　　　)</td></tr>
</table>

LEARN ENGLISH THROUGH PICTURES

Write the correct word(from the list below) to describe each picture:

(a) stairs /(b) binoculars /(c) surfing /(d) boots /(e) wall /(f) pier /(g) ferry /(h) map /(i) ruins /(j) monument

	( )		( )
	( )		( )
	( )		( )
	( )	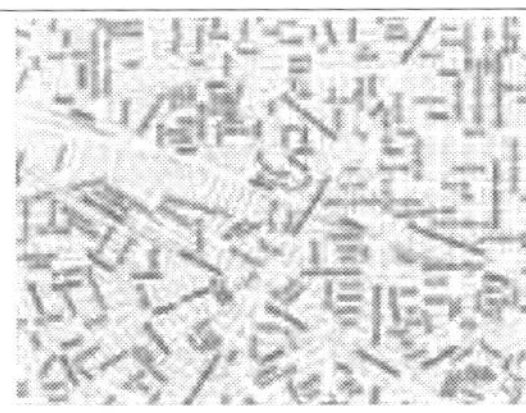	( )
	( )		( )

Exercise – ENGLISH FOR AIRPORT/AIRLINE CHECK-IN WORKERS

Fill in each blank with the correct word. If both words can be used, choose the one that sounds more natural in each situation:

1. How many _____(pieces/number) of luggage do you have?

2. The check-in doesn't start _____(for/until) another two hours.

3. So, you _____(missed/passed) your connecting flight because of the delay.

4. Since it was the airline's _____(fault/fall), we'll pay for your hotel and re-book your flight for tomorrow.

5. If you _____(cancellation/cancel) this ticket, you'll lose all your money. There is no refund for this type of ticket.

6. There's a special _____(shutter/shuttle) bus that goes/runs between Heathrow and Gatwick.

7. Are you traveling _____(alone/lonely)?(= by yourself)

8. The flight will be _____(boarding/boring) at(departure) gate 55.

9. There's an _____(overnight/reserved) flight that arrives in Vancouver at 8:00 AM.

10. What name was the reservation _____(under/over)?

Exercise – ENGLISH FOR AIRPORT/AIRLINE CHECK-IN WORKERS

Fill in each blank with the correct word. If both words can be used, choose the one that sounds more natural in each situation:

1. Do you have any _____(hand/arm) luggage?(= carry-on luggage)

2. That's a little too big to carry on the plane. You'll have to _____(give/check) it.

3. You flight _____(gets/makes) in(= arrives) at 7:00 PM.

4. Next in _____(line/line-up), please.

5. I'm going have to charge you for the _____(extra/extroverted)(= additional) bag.

6. Would you like a window seat or an _____(aisle/average) seat?

7. Baggage that's over the allowed limit = _____(Excess/Access) baggage

8. You should arrive at the gate no _____(later/late) than one hour before your flight.

9. I'm sorry - Your flight has been _____(cancelled/cancellation/cancel) because of bad weather.

10. Do you have your passport, or some other _____(form/format) of identification.

Exercise – ENGLISH FOR AIRPORT/AIRLINE CHECK-IN WORKERS

Fill in each blank with the correct word. If both words can be used, choose the one that sounds more natural in each situation:

1. You'll have to show the border guard your ticket and your _____(board/boarding) pass.

2. Did your flight arrive late? No, it actually arrived _____(ahead/front) of schedule.(= earlier than expected)

3. Because of the inconvenience, I'm going to _____(upgrade/upend)(= bump up) your ticket to first class.

4. How do you _____(spelling/spell) your name?

5. I'm going to have to _____(consult/console)(= discuss this) with my manager.

6. Did you check the lost and _____(found/find) to see if your bags are there?

7. Don't worry. Lost bags usually _____(show/shake) up(= appear) within 24 hours.

8. If someone or something is "behind schedule", it is _____(late/early).

9. The flight will be leaving on _____(hour/timetable/time).(= there won't be a delay)

10. You'll have to _____(hurry/fast) – They're almost finished boarding!

APPENDIX

APPENDIX

상황별 표현 복습 및 추가 정리

1. 예약에 관한 표현
① **I'd like to make a reservation.** 예약을 하고 싶습니다.
② **I'd like to book a flight for L.A.** L.A로 가는 비행기표를 예약하고 싶습니다.

2. 도움에 대한 감사의 표현
① **Thanks for all your help.**
② **I appreciate all your help.** 당신의 도움에 감사합니다.
③ **I can't thank you enough.** 어떻게 감사를 표해야할지 모르겠습니다.

3. 디저트를 거부할 때
① **I don't care for any dessert.**
② **I'll skip dessert.** 나는 어떤 디저트도 바라지 않습니다.

4. 계산에 대한 표현
① **I'll pay the bill.**
② **It's on me.**
③ **I'll treat you.** = This is my treat.
④ **Be my guest.** 제가 계산하겠습니다.
⑤ **Let's go Dutch.** 각자 내죠.

5. 후회의 감정을 나타내는 표현
① **I should have been more careful.** 내가 좀 더 신중했어야 했는데.
② **I should have done as you said.** 내가 당신이 말한 것처럼 했어야 했는데.

6. 용서/변명에 관한 표현
① **Will you forgive**(pardon, excuse) **me?** 나를 용서해 주시겠습니까?
② **Don't make excuse.** 변명 하지마.

7. 상대의 잘못에 대한 관용적 태도에 관한 표현

① **That's(It's) all right**. 괜찮습니다.

② **Don't worry about it**. 걱정 마세요.

8. 감정(기분)에 관한 표현

① **You look upset**. 당신은 언짢아 보입니다. cf) upset, angry, pissed off 화가난

② **Something seems to be bothering you**. 무엇인가 당신을 성가시게 하는 것 같습니다.

③ **I'm not in a good mood(in blue, in a bad humor)**.

④ **I'm a bit under the weather**. 나는 기분이 우울해요

⑤ **Keep your spirits up**. 기운 내

9. 짐을 부칠 때 쓰는 표현

① **A package must not exceed a certain size**. 짐은 정해진 사이즈를 초과하면 안 됩니다.

② **I would like to send this first class**. 나는 이것을 일등급으로 보내고 싶습니다.

10. 유감의 뜻을 나타내는 표현

① **It's a pity(shame, too bad) you don't speak standard English**. 유감스럽게도 당신은 표준 영어를 말하지 못합니다.

② **I wish I could**. ~했으면 좋았을걸

11. 목적지를 묻는 표현

① **Where are you headed for**? 어느 방향으로 가세요.

② **Where are you going**? 어디로 가십니까?

12. 동정적이나 수치스런 감정의 표현

① **That's too bad**. 참 안됐습니다.

② **That's a shame**. 수치스럽습니다. **cf) Shame on you**! 부끄러운지 알아라!

③ **It serves you right**. 꼴좋다.

13. 음식을 권유할 때

① **Please have some. Please try it**. 좀 드십시오.

② **Please help yourself(to it)**. 맘껏 드세요.

14. 식욕에 관한 표현

① **I have no trouble with my appetite**. 나의 식욕에는 아무런 문제도 없습니다.

② **The thought of the food makes me feel sick**. 그 음식 생각만 해도 아플 것 같습니다.

15. 상대방을 비하할 때 쓰는 표현

① **You're nuts**. 당신은 바보입니다. You're insane. * 바보 : fool, idiot, moron

② **You're out of your mind**. 당신은 제 정신이 아닙니다.

16. 상대방의 태도를 물을 때

① **Are you kidding**? 농담합니까?

② **Are you serious**? 진심입니까?

③ **What makes you think so**? 왜 그렇게 생각해.

④ **How come**? = What .... for? = why

17. 불확실한 것에 관한 표현

① **That would never happen**.

② **That's out of the question**. 그것은 전혀 불가능합니다.

18. 상대방의 말을 이해하지 못했을 때

① **I beg your pardon**. 다시 한 번 말씀해 주십시오.

② **I didn't hear you. I don't get it**. 당신의 말을 알아듣지 못했습니다.

19. 가격 인하에 관한 표현

① **It's on sale**. 그것은 세일 중입니다.

② **There's a big price reduction**. 대폭적인 가격 할인이 있었습니다.

20. 식당에서 사용되는 표현

① **Get whatever you want**. 당신이 원하는 것을 드세요.

② **Order whatever you want**. 당신이 원하는 것은 무엇이든 주문하세요.

③ **What would you like to have**? 무엇을 드시겠습니까?

④ **I'm full. I've had enough**. 충분히 먹었습니다. I'm stuffed. I'm good.

21. 가격에 관한 문의 표현

① **How much is the radio**?

② **What's the price of radio**?

③ **How much do I owe you**? 얼마죠?

④ **Will you pay by cash or credit card**? 현금입니까? 카드입니까? = Cash or charge?

22. 부재 중일 때의 표현

① **The doctor isn't in now.**

② **The doctor is out of the office right now.** 의사는 지금 안 계십니다.

23. 경제적 여유가 없을 때

① **I can't afford to buy a car.** 나는 차를 살 여유가 없습니다.

② **I have a limited budget.** 나는 월급쟁이입니다.

24. 도움을 주거나 요청할 때

① **What can I do for you?** 무엇을 도와 드릴까요?

② **Can I help you?** 도와 드릴까요?

③ **Could you give me a hand?** 저를 좀 도와주시겠어요?

④ **Mind if I ask a favor?** 부탁하나 할까요?

25. 만나기를 희망할 때

① **I'm looking forward to seeing you.**

② **I'm anxious to see you.** 나는 당신을 만나기를 학수고대합니다.

26. 상대방에게 무엇을 권할 때

① **Why don't you rent a car?**

② **How about renting a car?** 차를 빌리는 것이 어때요?

27. 은행에서 화폐를 교환할 때

① **I'd like to change won to dollars.** 저는 원화를 달러로 바꾸고 싶습니다.

② **I'd like to exchange dollars.** 저는 달러를 교환하고 싶습니다.

③ **I'd like to cash a check.** 현금을 수표로 바꾸고 싶은데요.

28. 요리의 익힌 정도를 말할 때

① **How would you like your stake?** 스테이크를 어떻게 해 드릴까요?

② **Rare, medium or well-done?** 조금, 중간, 많이 익힐까요?

29. 상대와 약속을 원할 때의 표현

① **I'd like to make an appointment to see the doctor.** 나는 의사의 진찰을 받기 위해서 약속을 하고 싶습니다.

30. 약속 가능한 시간을 말할 때의 표현

① **He's free on Tuesday at** 10:00. 그는 화요일 10시에 한가합니다.

② **He's available on Tuesday at** 10:00.

31. 상대의 근황을 물을 때의 표현

① **How are you getting along**?

② **How goes it**? 어떻게 지내십니까?

③ **How are things going**? **What's going on**? 잘 되어 갑니까?

④ **What's up**? **So-so**. 잘 지내세요? 그럭저럭이죠. Not bad!

⑤ **Say hello to, Give my regards to, Remember me to** ~안부 전해주세요

32. 허락을 요청할 때

① **Do you mind if I open the window**? 창문을 열어도 될까요?

② **Of course not. Not at all. No, I don't**. 그럼요. mind 응답에 주의

③ **Can I have your phone number if you don't mind**? 괜찮으시다면

33. 목적지까지 소요시간을 묻는 표현

① **How long will the bus take**? 버스로 얼마나 걸립니까?

② **How long does it take to get there**? 거기 도착하는 데 얼마나 걸립니까?

34. 기상에 관한 표현

① **What's the weather like for today**? 오늘 날씨는 어떻습니까?

② **The weather forecast for Seoul is partly cloudy**. 서울은 다소 구름이 끼겠습니다.

35. 주택에 관한 표현

① **What's your flat like**? 너의 아파트는 어떻게 생겼어?

② **Does the rent include utilities**? 임대료에는 공과금이 포함됩니까?

③ **How much security deposit do you require**? 보증금은 얼마입니까?

36. 가족에 대한 표현

① **My father is in his late** 40's. 나의 아버지는 40대 후반입니다.

② **I'm an only child**. 저는 독자입니다.

37. 전화에 관한 표현

① **Can I leave a message**? 말씀을 전해 주시겠어요?

② **Can you get me Kwangju** 361-5224? 361-5224번을 연결해 주세요.

③ **May I speak to Mr. Lee**? 이 군과 통화하고 싶은데요. * Is Lee there?

④ **Give me extension** 5966, **please**. 구내전화 5966번을 부탁합니다.

⑤ **I'll give you a call**(**phone, a ring**). 제가 전화하죠.

⑥ **Keep in touch once in a while**. 때때로 연락하며 삽시다.

⑦ **collect call** 수신자 부담통화

38. 부탁에 관한 표현

① **May I ask you a favor**? 부탁하나 해도 될까요?

② **Would you mind helping me with the dishes**? 설거지 좀 해 주시겠어요?

③ **I wonder if you can borrow your car**? 차좀 빌릴 수 있을까요?

39. 세탁에 관한 표현

① **Will you send this clothes to the laundry**? 이 옷을 세탁소에 보내 주시겠어요?

② **Two suits for dry cleaning**. 양복 두 벌을 드라이 클리닝 해 주세요.

40. 교통에 관한 표현

① **Is this train an express or a local**? 이 열차는 급행입니까, 완행입니까?

② **One way ticket or round trip ticket**? 편도입니까? 왕복입니까?

③ **Where should I transfer train**? 어디서 열차를 갈아타야 합니까?

④ **I'm going to get off at Fifth Avenue**? 5번가에서 내리겠습니다.

⑤ **How much is the taxi fare**? 택시 요금은 얼마죠? = taxi rate

⑥ **How far is it from the airport to the Hyatt Hotel**? 얼마나 멀죠?

⑦ **Keep the change, please**. 거스름돈은 가지세요.

41. 차량에 관한 표현 cf) Your car is fly. lemon(똥차)

① **There's a traffic jam**(=**congestion**) **down the road**. 도로가 정체되어 있습니다.

② **Fill it**(**her**) **up, please**. 기름을 가득 넣어주세요. cf) 만땅? gas tank

③ **I got a flat tire**. 타이어가 펑크났습니다.

④ **If you go over the speed limit, you'll get a ticket**. 과속하면 딱지를 뗍니다.

⑤ **gas station** 주유소, **change the battery** 배터리를 충전하다.

⑥ **pick up** 차에 태우다, **give a ride**(**lift**), **pull over/up** 차를 대다

* I will drop you off there. * 야 타! get in!, hop in!

42. 우편에 관한 표현

① **I'd like to send this by air mail.** 이것을 항공편으로 부치고 싶습니다.

② **How much is the postage?** 우편 요금은 얼마입니까?

43. 이발에 관한 표현 *ponytail, mohawk, cornrows

① **A little more off the back.** 뒷머리를 좀더 잘라 주십시오.

② **Trim my sideburns, please.** 양쪽 구레나룻을 손질해 주십시오.

③ **dye** 염색하다. **barber**(beauty salon) 이발소 **permanent** 파마

44. 촬영에 관한 표현 *DPE(development, printing, enlargement) 현상, 인화, 확대

① **Just develop the negatives.** 필름을 현상해 주십시오.

② **Please give me a roll of 35㎜ film.** 35밀리 필름을 주십시오.

③ **Will you enlarge this?** 이것을 확대해 주시겠어요?

45. 초대에 관한 표현

① **Won't you come and have dinner with us tomorrow?** 오셔서 함께 식사나 하지요.

② **Please help yourself to the cookies.** 과자를 드시죠.

46. 약국에 관한 표현

① **Where is the pharmacy?** 약국은 어디죠?

② **Can you prescribe some tranquillizer?** 진정제를 처방해 주실래요?

③ **Take two pills three times a day.** 하루에 세 번 알약 두 개를 복용하세요.

47. 길 묻기에 관한 표현

① **Can you tell me how to get to the Lotte Hotel?** 호텔에 가는 방법을 말해주세요.

② **I'm sorry. I'm a stranger here.** 미안합니다. 저도 여기가 처음입니다.

③ **Keep going straight. Turn right at the first corner.**

④ **You can't miss it.** 꼭 찾을 것입니다.

48. 항공 예약에 관한 표현

① **I'd like to reserve a seat on KAL Flight 201.** 대한항공 201편을 예약하고 싶습니다.

② **cancel** 예약취소, **reconfirmation** 예약 재확인

49. 기내에서의 표현

① **Which gate do I go to?** 어느 출입구로 가면 됩니까?

② **May I leave my belonging in this flight?** 제 휴대물을 기내에 두어도 됩니까?

50. 관광에 대한 표현

① **Could you tell me some interesting places**? 몇 군데 가 볼만한 곳이 있습니까?

② **Do you have a sightseeing brochure**? 관광안내 팜플렛이 있습니까?

51. 식당에서의 표현

① **What would you like to have**? 무엇을 드시겠습니까?

② **I'll have the same**. 저도 같은 것으로 주세요.

③ **What's 'Bulgogi' like**? 불고기는 어떤 것입니까?

④ **Could we have a table for three**? 3인분을 주시겠어요?

⑤ **Check, please**. 계산서 좀 주세요.

⑥ **Can we have separate bills**? 계산서는 따로따로 해 주세요

⑦ **Here or to go**? 여기서 드실 건가요, 싸드릴까요?

⑧ **Would you care for another one**? 더 드시겠어요? cf) After you. 먼저 드시죠

52. 비즈니스에 관한 표현

① **Could you type this report**? 이 보고서를 타이핑해 주시겠어요?

② **You should do the filing next**. 다음엔 서류철을 해야 합니다.

53. 옷가게에서의 표현

① **We're out of stock just now**. 우리는 지금 재고가 없습니다.

② **That becomes to you**. 이것은 당신에게 어울립니다.

③ **It looks as though it were made for you**. 이것은 당신을 위해 만든 것같이 보여요.

④ **loose** 옷이 헐렁하다. alter 옷을 고치다, hand washable 손빨래 가능

⑤ **shrink** 옷이 줄다 **I'm just looking**. 둘러보다, men' section 남성복 매장

⑥ **May I try it on**? 한 번 입어봐도 될까요? sold out 다 팔리다

54. 건강에 관한 표현

① **Please give me a first aid**. 응급조치를 해 주시오.

② **I've got a fever**. **My temperature is** 38 **degrees**. 38도의 고열입니다.

55. 가격에 관한 표현

① **Can't you make it a little cheaper**? 좀 깎아 주시면 안 될까요?

② **We can't take off a penny**. 우리 상점에서는 일원도 깎을 수 없습니다.

56. 파티에서 사용되는 표현

① **I haven't seen you for a long time. Long time no see.** 오랜만입니다. It has been a while.

② **How are you getting along these days?** 요즘 사업은 잘 되시죠?

③ **I'm afraid I've to leave now.** 이제 가 봐야겠습니다.

57. 약속에 관한 표현

① **He has got appointment all day on Monday.** 월요일은 약속으로 꽉 차 있습니다.

② **Anytime would be fine with me on that day.** 그날은 어느 때나 시간이 있습니다.

③ **postpone** 약속을 연기하다, **cancel** 취소하다, **make it** 시간 약속을 정하다

58. 만남, 작별에 대한 표현

① **What has brought you here?** 무슨 일로 여기에 왔어?

② **When shall we get together again?** 언제 다시 만나지?

③ **Drop me a line.** 편지해라

59. 감정에 대한 표현

① **How can you say such a thing?** 어떻게 그런 말을 할 수 있어?

② **Please leave me alone.** 제발 혼자 있게 해줘요.

③ **Don't bother me.** 괴롭히다. 폐 끼치다.(귀찮게 하다)

④ **We made up.** 우리 화해했어요.

60. 칭찬에 관한 표현

① **I'm not just flattering you.** 빈말하는 게 아냐.

② **He's the best tennis player I've ever seen.** 그는 제가 아는 사람 중 가장 테니스를 잘 쳐요.

③ **It can't be better.** 더 좋을 리 없다. 아주 좋다.

61.용서에 관한 표현

① **I didn't mean to hurt your feelings.** 당신의 감정을 상하게 할 의도는 아닙니다.

② **It couldn't be helped.** 어쩔 수 없었습니다.

62. 은행에 관한 표현

① **May I have money sent direct to my account?** 이 돈을 제 통장으로 입금해 주세요.

② **I'd like to open an account for myself.** 내 명으로 은행계좌를 개설하고자 합니다.

③ **interest** 이자, **withdraw** 인출하다, **deposit** 예금하다, **teller** 금전출납원

63. 상대방의 말에 동의할 때

① **You said it**. 바로 그래. 정말이야.

② **You can say that again**. 그럼. 그렇게 말 할 수 있지.

64. 상대방이 참견할 때

① **It's none of your business**.

② **Mind your own business**.

③ **Don't put your fingers in my pie**. 참견 하지 마

65. 기타

① **It's up to you**. 그것은 너에게 달려 있어.

② **If I had been in your shoes, I would have acted differently**. 내가 당신의 입장이라면, 다르게 행동했을텐데.

③ **Let me put it another way**. 그것을 달리 표현하고 싶어요.

④ **Take it easy**. 마음 편히 먹어. 여유를 가져.

⑤ **Make yourself at home**. 편히 쉬세요.

⑥ **Let's call it a day**. 오늘은 그만 하죠.

⑦ **What's on the tube(TV) tonight**? 오늘 밤 TV 프로는 뭐죠?

⑧ **There's no charge**. 무료입니다.

⑨ **I'm afraid I'm flat broke**. 저는 지금 빈털터리입니다.

⑩ **What's he like**? 그는 어떤 사람(성격)이죠?

Traffic Signs in the U.S.A.

※ 다음 영어로 된 표지판의 의미를 한국어로 표현해 봅시다.

Sign(s)	English	Korean
	Do Not Enter	"진입금지"
	No Parking	"______________"
	No Bicycles	"______________"
	No U Turn	"______________"
	No Left Turn	"______________"
	No Right Turn	"______________"
	No Parking Any Time	"______________"

<table>
<tr><th>Sign(s)</th><th>English</th><th>Korean</th></tr>
<tr><td>
</td><td>Stop</td><td>“정지”</td></tr>
<tr><td>
</td><td>Bicycle Lane</td><td>“______________”</td></tr>
<tr><td>
</td><td>Yield to oncoming traffic</td><td>“______________”</td></tr>
<tr><td>
</td><td>Speed Limit</td><td>“______________”</td></tr>
<tr><td>
</td><td>Minimum Speed Limit</td><td>“______________”</td></tr>
<tr><td>
</td><td>Reserved Parking for the Handicapped</td><td>“______________”</td></tr>
<tr><td>
</td><td>One Way Road</td><td>“______________”</td></tr>
</table>

직급의 한자/영자 표기

1. 會長 / 회장 / Chairman & CEO
2. 副會長 / 부회장 / Vice Chairman & CEO
3. 社長 / 사장 / President & COO
4. 副社長 / 부사장 / Senior Executive Vice President
5. 專務理事 / 전무이사, 전무 / Senior Managing Director & CFO
6. 常務理事 / 상무이사, 상무 / Managing Director
7. 理事 / 이사, 이사대우 / Director
8. 監事 / 감사 / Auditor General
9. 顧問 / 고문, 자문 / Advisor
10. 部長 / 부장 / General Manager
11. 本部長 / 본부장, 부장 / Director
12. 部長代理 / 부장대리 / Deputy General Manager
13. 次長 / 차장 / Deputy General Manager
14. 室長 / 실장 / General manager
15. 課長 / 과장 / Manager
16. 課長代理 / 과장대리 / Deputy manager
17. 代理 / 대리 / Assistant manager
18. 係長 / 계장 / Chief
19.主任 / 주임 / Assistant manager
20. 主任技士 / 주임기사 / staff engineer
21. 技士 / 기사 / Engineer
22. 首席研究員 / 수석연구원 / Principal Research Engineer
23. 責任研究員 / 책임연구원 / Senior Research Engineer
24. 先任研究員 / 선임연구원 / Research Engineer
25. 傳任研究員 / 전임연구원 / Associate Research Engineer
26. 主任研究員 / 주임연구원 / Assistant Research Engineer
27. 常任顧問 / 상임고문 / Executive Advisor
28. 專門委員 / 전문위원 / Research Fellow
20. 法務 / 법무팀 / Law Dept.
21. 戰略企劃 / 전략기획팀 / Plan Dept.
22. 海外事業 / 해외사업팀 / International Development Dept

'E-mail'상 주로 사용하는 영어표현

영문 이메일은 보통 영문의 편지문장과 몇 가지 차이가 있다. 가장 다른 점은 인포멀하고 간결한 문체일 것이다. 짧고, 친밀감을 담는 문체이지만 받는 사람에게 실례가 되지 않게 쓰지 않으면 안 된다. 이러한 어려움 때문에 지금까지는 영문으로 전자메일을 쓰려고 생각해도 부담이 되어서 쓰기를 망설였던 사람들이 많을 것이다. 그런 분들을 위해서 영문 e-mail에 자주 나오는 편리한 표현을 오랜 작업 끈에 정리해 보았다. 이러한 표현을 참고하셔서 이제는 주저하지 마시고 짧아도 괜찮으니 영문 e-mail를 한번 써 보자.

* 자기소개의 표현

- **I'm sending this mail from Seoul, Korea.** 한국의 서울에서 메일을 보냅니다.
- **This is my first mail to send to this mailing list.** 이 메일링 리스트에 처음으로 메일을 보냅니다..
- **I work for a multimedia company that makes educational software.**
  교육용 소프트를 만드는 회사에서 근무하고 있습니다.
- **I am Bonghee Han from Daejeon-City, Korea.** 한국의 대전시에서 살고 있는 한 봉희라고 합니다.

* 인사 표현

- **How have you been(doing)? Nothing much new here.** 안녕하십니까. 이곳은 별다른 일없습니다.
- **I'm happy to join this movie lover's mailing list.** 이 영화 동호인 메일일 리스트에 가입되어 영광입니다.
- **I sent e-mail to you last weekend but I guess I sent it to the wrong address.**
  제가 지난주에 메일을 보냈습니다만 잘못된 주소에 보낸 것 같네요.

* 감사의 표현

- **Thanks for your quick reply(Response).** 빠른 답장 감사합니다.
- **Thank you for your e-mail dated April** 15, 2001. 2001년 4월 15일자 메일 고맙습니다.
- **If you could take a few minutes to answer our questions, we would really appreciate it.**
  저희들의 질문에 시간을 조금만 내서 답변을 해 주신다면 감사하겠습니다.
- **Thank you in advance for your help.** 아무쪼록 부탁 드립니다.(미리 감사드립니다.)

* 사죄의 표현

- **Sorry I didn't write to you earlier.** 좀 더 빨리 쓰지 못해 죄송합니다.
- **I apologize for not having gotten into contact with you sooner.** 좀 더 빨리 연락을 드리지 못해서 죄송합니다.
- **Sorry for any confusion and it is a pleasure doing business with you.**
  혼란스럽게 해서 죄송합니다. 그리고 당신과 비즈니스를 같이하게 되어 기쁩니다.

* 제안의 표현

- **I'd like to make a proposal: Why don't we write our messages all in English?**
  제안이 있습니다. 우리는 왜 메시지를 전부 영어로 쓰지 않습니까?
- **Are you interested in going to a baseball game with me this weekend?**
  이번 주말에 저와 야구하러 가는 것에 관심이 있습니까?
- **Why don't you stop by Korea if you are coming to Japan?** 일본에 온다면 한국에도 들러 주세요!

* 문의의 표현

- **Does anyone know if those movies are available on videotape?**
  이러한 영화가 비디오테이프로 가능할지 누가 모릅니까.
- **I need your help.** 도와주세요.
- **When can I expect a reply from you?** 언제 답장을 받아 볼 수 있을까요!.
- **I just want to check if you have received my mail of April 23rd.**
  4월 23일 보낸 나의 메일을 받으셨는지 확인하고 싶습니다.
- **Is there anybody out there who has the last month's English Network?**
  누군가 지난 달의 영어 네트워크를 갖고 계시지 않습니까?

* 답변의 표현

- **I am responding to your job opening announcement in the Korea Times dated April 5th.**
  4월 5일자의 코리아 타임즈 구인광고 건으로 연락하고 있습니다.
- **Here is my answer to your question of April 1st.** 4월 1일자의 당신 질문에 대한 답변입니다.
- **I wish I could go, but I have already made plans on the 12th.**
  갈 수 있으면 좋겠습니다만, 벌써 12일에는 계획이 있습니다.
- **Hope this helps.** 이것이 도움이 되길 기대합니다.

* 의뢰의 표현

- **I hate to ask you this, but would it be possible for us to stay with you?**
  이러한 것을 부탁드리기가 싫지만 당신과 함께 머무르는 것이 가능할까요?
- **Let me know the results of your entrance exams in the next mail.** 다음 메일로 입시의 결과를 가르쳐 주세요.
- **Could you help me with my survey?** 나의 조사에 답해 주실 수 있겠습니까?
- **May I ask a favor of you?** 부탁을 해도 될까요?
- **I am looking for key-pals in Mexico, Spain or South America.**
  멕시코와 스페인과 남아메리카에서 전자메일로 펜팔할 상대를 찾고 있습니다.
- **We would like to e-mail with an elementary school class in Italy.**
  이탈리아의 초등학교 클래스와 전자메일을 교환을 하고 싶습니다.
- **Please respond to iambong@netsgo.com** 연락은 iambong@netsgo.com 로 주세요!

* 확인의 표현

- **Did you mention you wanted to start this business by March this year or March next year?** 이 비즈니스를 금년 3월까지 시작하기로 언급했습니까? 아니면, 내년 3월까지라고 언급했습니까?.
- **Did you also say we need a unix machine for this?** 당신은 또한 UNIX의 컴퓨터가 필요하다고 말했습니까?

* 감정의 표현

- **I'm a bit disturbed by your reply to our new product.** 저희들의 상품에 대해서 당신의 답변에 놀랐습니다.
- **I'm so glad/happy that you liked our gift.** 당신이 우리의 선물을 좋아하시니 기쁩니다.
- **I'm terribly sorry to hear of Dr. Johnson's sudden death.** 존슨 선생님의 갑작스런 죽음을 듣고 놀랐습니다. 명복을 빕니다.

* 축하의 표현

- **I wish you the best of luck /good luck with your final exams.** 기말 시험에서의 행운을 빕니다.
- **How are you feeling? I heard you couldn't come to work for several days because you got sick.** 상태는 어떻습니까. 병이 들어 몇 일간 출근을 못한다고 들었습니다.
- **Have a good rest until you feel completely well.** 완전히 좋아질 때까지 충분히 휴양을 취하세요.
- **I'm really glad to hear you got promoted.** 당신의 승진을 진심으로 축하드립니다.
- **Congratulations on your marriage!** 결혼 축하합니다.
- **You deserve to get promoted.** 당신의 승진은 당연합니다.

* E-mail 주세요

- **E-mail me or call me collect, please.** 전자메일이나 콜렉트콜로 연락 주세요.
- **Hope to here from you soon.** 당신으로부터 빠른 답장을 기다리고 있습니다.
- **I'm looking forward to receiving your reply at your earliest convenience.** 가능한 한 빨리 답장을 받을 수 있기를 학수 고대하고 있습니다.
- **Please send responses by the end of April.** 4월 말까지 답장을 주세요.

* 마지막 한마디

- **I'll tell you more about it in my next message.** 다음 메일로 좀 더 이야기를 하겠습니다.
- **I'll keep in touch.** 연락을 합시다.
- **Please give my best regards to your boss.** 당신의 상사에게 안부 전해 주십시오.

* 아래는 E-mail에서 자주 나오는 약어

네트워크를 이용하는 User들은 가능한 한 문장을 짧게 쓰기 위해서 이러한 특수한 약어를 낳았다. 익숙해질 때까지는 너무 자주 사용하는 것은 권장하지 않지만, 읽었을 때 어떠한 의미인지 정도를 이해할 수 있도록 알아두자. 그리고 한두 개 정도는 이메일에 사용해 보아도 좋을 것이다.

▶기본적인 약어

P. S. / Post Script 추신
BTW / By the way 그런데
ASAP / As soon as possible 가능한 한 빨리
co. / company 회사
et al. /(et alia 라틴어로부터) and others 그 외
i.e. /(id est 라틴어로부터) that is 즉
e.g. /(exempli garatia 라틴어로부터) for example 예를 들면

▶화재를 바꾼다

OBTW / Oh, By The Way 그런데
OTOH / On The Other Hand 한편
AFAIC / As Far As I'm Concerned 나에 관해서 말하면
IOW / In Other Words 즉
IAC / In Any Case 어쨌든

▶마지막 인사

CIAO / Goodbye(이탈리아어) 안녕
CUL / See You Later 다시 또 보자
CWYL / Chat With You Later 또 이야기합시다
TTYL / Talk To You Later 또 이야기하네요
BFN / Bye for now 오늘은 이 정도로

▶컴퓨터 용어

HDD / Hard Disk Drive 하드 디스크
Msg / Message e-mail 문장
Cc / carbon copy 참조(같은 것을 다른 사람에게도 보내는 기능)
Bcc / Blind carbon copy 숨은 참조(상대에게는 알리지 않고 같은 것을 다른 사람에게도 보내는 기능)
KBD / Keyboard 키보드
Snail Mail / The U.S. Postal Service 우편(우편은 전자 메일에 비해 달팽이처럼 늦기 때문에)

▶프로만 아는 생략어

IITYWTMWYKM / If I Tell You What This Means Will You Kiss Me?
HHO 1/2 **K** / Ha, Ha, Only Half Kidding 좀 농담을 했다니까!
ROFLASTC / Rolling On Floor Laughing And Scaring The Cat! 배꼽이 빠지게 웃는다
WYSIWYG / What You See Is What You Get 모니터에 보이는 대로 인쇄된다
IMHO / In My Humble Opinion 사견을 말하면
IMO / In My Opinion 생각건대
FYI / For Your Information 도움이 될꺼라고 생각해

▶상대를 어리석게 하는 것

KISS / Keep It Simple, Stupid 간단하게 못하니, 바보야!
IMNSHO / In My No So Humble Opinion 말하게 해주지만
LLTA / Lots and Lots of Thunderous(or Thundering) Applause 박수 갈채
RTFM / Read The F＊cking Manual! / Read The Flaming Manual! 메뉴얼을 읽어라.

▶위트

HAK / Hugs And Kisses (꼭 껴안고 키스해줄 정도로) 훌륭하다!
ROFL/ROTFL / Rolling On Floor Laughing! 박장대소하다
HHOK / Ha, Ha, Only Kidding 농담이야.
ONNA / Oh No, Not Again 좀 기다려요.
OZ / Australia 오스트레일리아(사람)

▶감사

THANX / TNX Thanks 고맙습니다
TIA / Thanks In Advance 잘 부탁드립니다

▶기 타

HTH / Hope this Helps! 이것이 도움이 될거야!
FYA / For Your amusement 이것으로 즐기세요
FYI / For your information 정보입니다
WT / Without Thinking 너무 생각하지 말고

감정을 그림 문자로 표현하는 마크도 생략 기호의 하나이다. 적절히 사용하면 매우 효과적이다. 많이 사용하는 것을 모아 보았다.

^_^) smile (^_^; embarrassed \^_^/ banza-i :-) Happy

:@ what? :D Laughter :I Hmmm... :(Sad

:O Yelling :,(Crying :* Kisses (:-) smiley big-face

;-) wink -) hee hee -(mad

Clothes

English	Korean	English	Korean
sweats	운동복	jeans	청바지
flip flop	쪼리	cardigan sweater	가디건
jacket	자켓	baggy pants	힙합바지
boxer shorts shorts	사각 팬티 짧은 바지	tank top	(수영복처럼 생긴) 여성용 상의
dress shirt (Y-shirt)	와이셔츠	bell bottoms	나팔바지
stockings	스타킹	striped	줄무늬의
polka-dotted	물방울 무늬의	checked	체크무늬의
plaid	격자무늬의	floral	꽃무늬의
fitting room	탈의실	turtleneck sweater	목(neck)부분까지 올라오는 스웨터
skirt	스커트, 치마	bow tie	나비넥타이
leggings	쫄바지	trousers	바지
suit	정장(양복)	overcoat	코트(외투)
vest(undershirt)	조끼(속옷)	sweater	스웨터(점퍼)

Currency

<table>
<tr><th>지폐모양</th><th>지폐의 이름</th><th colspan="2">주요 사용 국가</th></tr>
<tr><td></td><td>United States
Dollar</td><td colspan="2">U.S.A</td></tr>
<tr><td></td><td>Canada Dollar</td><td colspan="2">Canada</td></tr>
<tr><td></td><td>Euro</td><td>Finland
Ireland
Portugal
Greece
Luxembourg
Netherlands</td><td>Germany
France
Spain
Italy
Austria
Belgium</td></tr>
<tr><td></td><td>Pound</td><td colspan="2">U.K.</td></tr>
<tr><td></td><td>Yen</td><td colspan="2">Japan</td></tr>
<tr><td></td><td>Yuan</td><td colspan="2">China</td></tr>
</table>

Currency of the U.S.

	1달러 ☞ 한화 약 1,100원 ☞ 조지 워싱턴의 초상화(초대 대통령)		100달러 ☞ 한화 약 110,000원 ☞ 벤자민 프랭클린의 초상화
	2달러 ☞ 한화 약 2,200원 ☞ 토머스 제퍼슨의 초상화 (3대 대통령)		Penny(페니=센트) ☞ 1 cent (한화 10원 정도) ☞ 앞면 → 링컨 대통령 뒷면 → 링컨 기념관
	5달러 ☞ 한화 약 5,500원 ☞ 아브라함 링컨의초상화 (16대 대통령)		Nickel(니켈) ☞ 5 cent (한화 50원 정도) ☞ 앞면→제퍼슨 대통령 뒷면→제퍼슨 기념관
	10달러 ☞ 한화 약 11,000원 ☞ 헤밀턴 (초대재무장관)의 초상화		Dime(다임) ☞ 10 cent (한화 100원 정도) ☞ 앞면 → 루즈벨트 대통령 뒷면 → 자유의 횃불
	20달러 ☞ 한화 약 22,000원 ☞ 잭슨의 초상화 (7대 대통령)		Quarter(쿼터) ☞ 25 cent (한화 250원 정도) ☞ 앞면→조지워싱턴 뒷면→독수리
	50달러 ☞ 한화 약 55,000원 ☞ 그랜트의 초상화 (18대 대통령)	※미국의 지폐는 색깔과 크기가 모두 동일합니다. 또한 특정 지역에서는 1달러짜리 동전을 사용하기도 합니다.	

영어 욕설 (*어느 정도의 영어 욕을 알아야 대화가 된다)

(swear words, curses, dirty words...) Anderson Lee's lessons 욕 강의 동영상 참조

욕은 offensive(다른 사람의 기분을 상하게 하는)하기 때문에 가급적 남 앞에서는 안 하는게 좋지만 가끔은 한 번 후련하게 욕해주고 나면(그래도 싼 인간들에게) 스트레스가 확 풀리곤 한다. 그런 인간들에게 욕 하나도 제대로 못해준다면 그 홧병이 속으로 쌓일테니까. 개인적으로는 DJ doc의 노래를 좋아하는 이유가 거기에 있다.

기본 욕 3가지(동영상에서 강의하는 내용임)

1. sick *욕 아님 = 쩔어, 젊은이들이 아주 좋거나 나쁠 때
   영어에서는 주로 좋을 때
   The weather is sick. Your skin is sick. 할아버지 피부가 쩔어요.
2. asshole 똥구멍, 한국 초딩이 쓰면(욕?), 영어권 모두 씀
3. son of bitch(cf. beach) 여자 : bitch You bitch!

영어 욕의 꽃

4. fuck What the fuck!
5. fucking

4. 5 + 1, 2, 3 으로 합쳐 씀

Your English is fucking sick.
Your dancing is fucking sick.
She is fucking cute.

영어 욕설에 대한 정리

1. Fuck

sex의 은어로서 영어권에서 가장 심한 욕이다. 방송에서 언제나 편집되며 친구들 사이에서도 웬만하면 쓰지 않는 욕이다. 가운데 손가락을 세우는 특유의 행위와 연관이 된다. 내 친구는 중학교 때 미국 유학가서 멋 모르고 옆 짝꿍에게 'Fuck you' 라는 말과 함께 가운데 손가락을 세웠다가 바로 부모님 소환 당하고 교장과 면담했다. 그러니 자제하길 바란다. 총 맞는다.^^ 연관되는 욕으로, 'Fuck you~!', 'What the fuck(WTF)', 'mother fucker' 등이 있다.

2. suck

suck는 사전상 '빨다'라는 뜻으로, 사실상 fuck와 유사한 의미를 내포하고는 있지만 그렇게 심한 욕은 아니다. 사용되는 의미는 한국에서 사용하는 '내 발바닥이나 핥아라.' 정도의 의미로서 '형편없는, 상대가 안 되는' 정도의 의미를 가지고 있다. cf) You suck!!! 반대말 - rock? 연관되는 욕으로. 'sucker', 'Can you dig it sucker~?' 정도가 있다. 그래서 'you suck!'(의역하면 이 나쁜놈아! 또는 넌 정말 아냐..) 사물이 주어일 때는 rain sucks!(비오는 거 정말 싫어!) 정도의 의미가 있다.

3. ass

ass는 엉덩이, asshole은 항문의 의미이다. 영어에서 가장 빈번하게 욕의 소재로 사용되는 신체부위가 엉덩이이다. 그에 반하면 우리가 좀 더 노골적이긴 하다. 남자나 여자나 ㅈ(사전상의 의미는 어른 남성의 성기)을 입에 달고 사니깐.^^(한국 사는 외국인들이 가끔 ㅈ나, ㅈ도, ㅈ되네 같은게 뭐냐고 물어보는 경우가 있는데. 상세히 알려주면 기겁을 한다. ㅋㅋ) 연관되는 욕으로. 'Kick your ass~!'(엉덩이를 걷어 차주마 - 우리나라에서 쓰는 '다리 몽뎅이를 뿐질러 주마' 와 비슷한 아주 흔한 관용어이다), 'kiss my ass~!'(엉덩이에 뽀뽀를 해라~! - 우리나라에서 쓰는 '놀고들 있네', '웃기시네', ' 알랑방귀를 뀐다 '정도의 의미이다.) 정도가 있다.

4. damn

damn이라는 것은 혼잣말로 상태의 안 좋음을 표현할 때 주로 사용하는 편이다. 상대에게 쓰는 경우는 그리 많지 않은 편이다. 우리나라에서 빌어먹을 정도의 의미를 가지고 있다. 연관되는 욕으로. 'damn it~!', 'god damn' 등이 있다.

5. crap

영어권에서, 특히 미국에서 욕으로 자주 사용된다. '망치다, 흡집내다, 불평하다, 할퀴다' 정도의 파괴적이고 공격적인 의미를 가지고 있는 단어로서, 주로 우리나라에서 '젠장' 정도의 느낌으로 자주 사용되는 편이다. 역시 혼잣말로 사용되는 경우가 많다.

6. bitch

'마녀, 악녀, 미친년' 정도의 의미가 있는 단어이다. 은어로 '쫄개, 꼬붕, 시다' 정도의 의미도 가지고 있다. 대부분 bitch 앞에 교활한, 음란한, 방정맞은, 음탕한, 형편없는 같은 어휘가 붙어서 의미를 풍성하게 해준다. 연관되는 욕으로 'son of a bitch'가 있는데 우리나라에서 '개새끼'로 번역될 만큼 관용적인 욕이다. son of~! 까지만 하는 경우도 많다.

7. loser

말 그대로 '패배자'이다. '병신, 낙오자'의 의미를 담고 있다.

8. jackass

'당나귀 새끼'라는 뜻을 가지고 있다. '멍청이'란 의미로 사용되지만 우리나라의 '짜식, 임마' 정도의 느낌도 있는 편이다.

9. idiot

'백치'라고 정의된다. 우리나라의 '등신'이라는 의미로 자주 사용된다. 어원은 그리스 어 이디오테스(idiotes)에서 온것으로 '남과 다른' '특별한' 이라는 뜻이라고 한다. → idiot, moron, dumb ass 전부 '지능이 떨어지는 사람'의 의미가 있다. ex) Do you think I'm an idiot?(너 내가 바보인줄 알아?)

10. stupid

'멍청이'라는 뜻이다. 어원은 라틴 어 스투피두스(stupidus) 에서 온 것으로 '놀라운 일을 당해서 어리둥절하다' 라는 뜻이다.

11. shit

'대변, 똥' 이라는 뜻이다. 역시 사용빈도가 높은 욕이다. damn, shit, crab 삼총사가. 안 좋은 의미로서의 감탄사로 자주 사용된다. 우리나라의 '젠장', '빌어먹을', '썅~!' 정도의 느낌이다. 연관되는 욕으로 'bullshit' 이라는 욕이 있는데 직역하면 '소똥'이고, ^^ 의역하면 '헛소리', '웃기지 마'라는 의미가 있다.

12. shut up

'닥쳐라'는 관용어이다. '조용히 해'라는 의미보다는 '닥쳐'라는 욕설의 의미가 강하다. 하지만 요새 미국에서는 친한 친구들 사이에서 '설마(?)' 정도의 느낌으로 사용되기도 한다.

13. fool

foolish라고도 하며 '바보'라는 의미이다. 욕 중에서 가장 충격이 약한 욕이고 그래서 책이나 방송에서 가장 많이 사용되는 편이다. '덜 떨어진' 이라는 의미의 fool, stupid, idiot 중에서 가장 의미가 약한 편이다.(idiot 가장 욕설로서 의미 전달이 강력하다!! 순서대로 바보, 멍충이, 등신이라고 보면 된다.^^)

14. bastard

'망나니'라는 의미의 단어이다. 정확한 사전적 의미는 '사생아'이다. '사상아, 서출의, 잡종의, 거짓의, 개자식' 이라고 정의되어 있다. 연관되는 욕으로는 'Luck bastard' 가 있는데, 욕이라기 보다는 우리나라에서 '운 좋은 새끼' 라는 느낌으로 친구들 사이에서 쓰인다. → jerk, jack ass, bastard 보통 남자를 지칭하는 말입니다. 무슨 뜻인지는 다 아실테니까...

ex) He's a real jerk!(정말 나쁜 놈이야…)

기타

→ chicks

chick은 바로 '어린 닭', 즉 '병아리'라는 의미이다. 바로 '어린 여자'를 가리키는 말이다. 우리말로 하면 '영계'쯤 된다. 여자들이 들으면 기분 나쁘겠죠? 여자들이 좋아하는 멜로 영화(시애틀의 잠 못 이루는 밤이나 노팅 힐 같은)를 chick flicks라고 합니다. flick는 '영화'라는 뜻이다.

→ **chickens(=coward)**

닭이 왜 이런 오명을 쓰고 있는지는 모르겠지만 '겁쟁이' 또는 '비겁한 사람'의 의미가 있다. 영화 '흐르는 강물처럼'에서 급류를 타려는 브래드 피트가 망설이는 친구들 앞에서 닭 날개짓을 하며 닭 소리를 내죠. 빠박 빡빡빡!

→ **Holy 시리즈**

욕에 왜 holy(성스러운)을 붙이는지 이해는 안 가지만 아무튼…

Holy cow! '이런!' 정도의 의미로 어린 아이들 앞에서도 쓸 수 있는 말

Holy crap! TV에서도 들을 수 있는 말이지만 역시 점잖은 말은 아니다.

Holy shit! 아마 TV에서는 shit 부분이 삐~~ 하고 검열될 것이다.

→ **Oh my God! Jesus Christ!**

무언가에 깜짝 놀라서(주로 안 좋은 일) 내뱉는 말로서 '세상에', '맙소사' 정도의 의미이다. 예를 들면, 자동차에 치일 뻔 했다든지 야구공이 바로 옆을 스치고 지나갔다든지 하는 일들…. 하지만 기독교인들은 이런 말을 싫어한다. 불쾌한 감정을 나타내는 말로 하나님과 예수님의 이름을 사용하는 것이니까. 따라서 기독교인들 앞에서는 이 말을 삼가하는 것이 좋다. 일반인들 사이에서는 아주 빈번하게 사용된다.

⊙사람이 살다보면 남에게 욕을 하는 경우가 있죠. 뭐, 자주 그러면 안 되겠지만 …
이번에는 사람을 지칭하는 욕에 대해서 알아봅시다.(그렇다고 외워서 쓰지는 말자구요..^^;;)

→ **whore**

원래는 '창녀'라는 의미로 여자에게 쓰는 말이겠죠?

*현지에서 가장 잘 쓰이는 욕들입니다 … 20세 이하 외우지 마시오(경고)

- Fag = 계집애
- faggot = fag랑 비슷
- douche(듀쉬 라고 읽음) = 얼간이
- jackass = 멍청이
- fatass = 뚱돼지
- douche bag = 얼간이(실제로는 성인용품인가? 그런 거라는 데 욕으로 씀)
- dumbass = 멍청이
- dumbshit = 멍청이
- dick
- dickhead
- dickhole
- cock = dick이랑 같음
- cunt = 여자 dick

- pussy= cunt랑 같음
- vagina = cunt랑 같음
- vulva = cunt랑 같음
- boobs = 가슴
- titties = 젖꼭지
- nipple = 젖꼭지
- Jew = 유대인 비하하는 식으로 부르는 것
- chink = 짱깨(중국인 비하하는 식으로 부르는 것)
- jap = 쪽바리(일본인 비하하는 식으로 부르는 것)
- nigger = 깜댕이(흑인비하) ★이거 절대 흑인한테 하면 안댐. 했다간 맞아죽을지도 모름 the black = the colored = negro
- idiot = ㅂㅅ
- what the heck,
- what the hell (이것들은 다른 것에도 응용가능) 예) why the fuck are you here?(너 ㅅㅂ 여기 왜 있어) 등등
- what the fuck
- bullshit = 구라쟁이, 구라까다 등등
- piss off = 꼴받게 하다(열받게 하다) ex) I'm fucking pissed off.
- screw off = screw you
- son of bitch = 개자식
- imbecile = 저능한, 바보
- schmuck = 얼간이
- shut the fuck up = 닥쳐
- shut up = 닥쳐
- moron = 저능아
- take a hike = 꺼져
- screwbal = 쓸모없는 사람
- Don't be vulgar = 상스럽게 굴지마
- beggar = 거지
- bone head = 돌대가리
- Shut the fuck up, creep = 닥쳐, 벌레 같은 놈아
- homicide = 살인자
- Lunatic = 미치광이
- Dingbat = 머저리

⊙ 그리고 이것들은 욕은 아니지만 채팅에서 자주 쓰이는 말이다

- lol = laugh out loud '큰소리로 웃다' 이런 뜻.
- lmao = laugh my ass off '엉덩이 떨어질 만큼 웃다' 이런 뜻?
- rofl = rolling on the floor laughing(맞나?) '웃겨서 땅바닥 구른다' 뭐 대충 이런 뜻
- roflmao = rofl 과 lmao 의 합체버젼 ㅋㅋ

위트 넘치는 영어 표현

⊙ 네이티브 스피커들은 간단하면서도 직설적이지 않은, 감정이 덜 섞인 표현들을 좋게 생각한다.

1. 위트 넘치는 비유 표현들

- 힘에 부친다. out of one's hand
- 누구 손에 달렸다. be in one's hands
- 현실을 받아 들여라. Let's face it.
- 확실하다(불보듯 뻔하다). as plain as the nose on your face
- 서로 돕자. You scratch my back, I'll scratch yours.
- 사소한데 집착하다(목숨 걸다). split hairs
- 운 나쁜 날. bad hair day
- 일진이 안 좋은. got off on the wrong foot today, got out of the wrong side of the bed, this is no my day, this is not my lucky day.
- 식은죽 먹기. it was like taking candy from a baby
- 아주 쉽다. don't sweat it, no sweat
- 변하지 않는. die hard, never change
- 실패로 끝난 일. go down the tubes, go up in smoke
- 이러지도 저러지도 못하다. be on the rocks, between a rock and a place, I'm damned if I do and damned if I don't
- 문득 생각나다. ring a bell, got it
- 아주 바쁘다. tied up, My hands are full, I don't have enough time to think, I'm so busy i don't know what direction i'm headed,
- 냉대를 받다. cold shoulder
- 게으르게 뒹굴거리는 사람. couch potato, veg out around the house
- 푹자. sleep tight
- 행운이 계속되길 바래. knock on wood
- 잘 됐으면 좋겠다. keep your fingers crossed, cross your fingers.
- 약속 합니다. I give you my word, cross my heart, hope to die, stick a needle in my eye, I promise
- 포기 하지마. stick to ~
- 실패도 재산이야(좋은 공부가 됐을거야. 댓구법). you live, you learn
- 다른 댓구 표현의 예. you lie, you die. you talk, you walk.
- 준비완료. all systems go
- 선착순!! First come, first served. It's first come. First-come basis. First-come system.
- 불행과 분노를 달랠 때. It's not the end of the earth.

2. 네이티브의 콧대를 납작하게 하는 말들

- 꿈깨. Get real!
- 구제불능이다. You never learn.
- 당연한거 아냐? What do you expect?
- 말려도 듣지 않아서 멋대로 해라고 할 때. It's your funeral.
- 어쩔 수 없다고 할 때. Water under the bridge.
- 충고를 듣지 않을 때. Suit yourself, Have it your way.
- 대답하고 싶지 않은 질문에는. Maybe yes, maybe no.
- 우유부단한 친구에게. That's your problem, It's up to you, The decision is up to you.
- 쓸데없는 질문에 댓구할 때. Who knows?, I don't know, Good question, Why are you asking me? How should I know?
- 지각한 사람에게 한마디 할 때. Better late than never.

3. 회의와 협상의 말들

- 뒷일은 당신에게 달렸어요. The ball's in your court, It's(all)up to you, It's your responsibility now.
- 마지막 카드를 제시할 때. Take it or leave it.
- 깨진 협상을 마무리 할 때. We agree to disagree on this.
- 일의 진전을 표현할 때. So far, so good. Pretty good(not very good, nothing's gone right), so far.
- 잘못된 것을 지적할 때 우회적으로. I must be missing something. I'm not clear on something. I'm getting confused.
- 의견을 애매하게 받아 넘길 때. I appreciate your insight.
- 얼버무릴 때. I'll take it under consideration. I'll think about it. I'll give it some serious thought.
- 빠른 일처리를 부탁할 때. The sooner, the better.
- 비관적인 사람에게. We'll cross that bridge when we get to it.
- 우선순위에 관한 말들. first things first
- 낙관이나 비관을 경계할 때. let's hope for the best and prepare for the worst. hope is not a solution.
- 비즈니스 경구. think slowly, act quickly. think ahead and don't rush. think big but start small. more haste, less speed.

4. 간단해도 뉘앙스까지 전하는 말들

- 감탄사로. man 긍정적 의미, boy 긍정 부정적 의미(아~)
- 부가의문문 처리. huh? excuse me. pardon. what was that? please say that again. one more time, please?
- 여운을 주면서 표현하는. well. 저~, 어~, 아~, 음~, 앗~
- 사려 깊은 사람이 되고 싶을 때. oh~ 네, 앗, 아, 오
- 웬만한 부탁은 요걸로. do me a favor
- 말문이 막힐 때 시간을 버는. ah, uh, mm, you know…
- 리스닝의 문제네(그게 뭐더라, 그거 말이야). What do you call it?
- '그럴지도 몰라요' 라고 얼버무릴 때. I never know. no one knows. Who knows.

• 그저 그래(better). been(seen, toasted) better
그저 그래(worse). been(seen, toasted) worse
• 말바꾸거나 고칠 때. I mean. You mean.
• 의심스러운 말에 대꾸할 때. I'll believe it when I see it. I'd like to see it with my own eyes.
• 귀찮은 사람을 정중히 물리칠 때. spare me. leave me alone. don't bother(bug) me.
• 맘상하지 않게 상대를 꾸짖을 때. That's so unlike you.
• 결톤에 따라서도 의미가 달라지는. great(대단해, 심하군), you heard me(들렸어?, 얼버무리지마), very funny(재밌다, 재미없다)
• 화제를 바꾸거나 매듭질 때. well. okay. all right.
• 뭔가를 알아채고 말할 때. now(자, 그런데, 이봐, 그럼, 그렇지)
• 믿거나 말거나. believe it or not
• 조심스럽게 의견을, 어느 쪽인가 하면. I guess

5. 부탁 거절 변명을 세련되게 하는 말들

• 내가 원하는 바를 부드럽게 돌려서. It might(could) be better if…
• 상대가 원하는 바를 부드럽게 돌려서. You might want to…
• 부탁을 어른스럽게 거절할 때. I would if I could, but I can't.
• 세련되게 충고할 때. If I were you… You might think about…
• 성격이나 특징을 추측해서 말할 때. You must be…
• 다음에 할게요. rain check
• 가벼운 부탁. I was wondering if you'd…
• 나쁜 뜻은 없었어. Don't get me wrong. I didn't mean to. Don't misunderstand me. · Don't get the wrong impression. It's nothing personal.
• 부드럽게 말할 때(주어 옆에). I ah. You ah. We ah. It's ah. She's ah
• 형편을 말할 때. afford

6. 품격을 높여주는 말들

• 프라이버시를 물을 때. Could I ask? / Do you mind if i ask?
• 실례지만. May(might) i ask?
• 격식을 갖춰서. indeed가 very, really 보다 좋아
• 설득력을 높여주는. perhaps, maybe
• 단호한 의견을 부드럽게. I find it…
• 좋고 싫음을 품위 있게 표현할 때. be not keen on
• 세련되게 권할 때. you must / you should
• 품위 있는 여성이 쓰면 좋은. lovely
• 이름이 생각이 나지 않을 때. Your name has slipped my tongue. You're … is on the tip of my tongue. You're let me see. Your name is… I've misplaced your name card. Do you have an extra with you?
• 교양 있게 남을 평가하는. on the … side

- 귀여운 여인의 감탄사. why(어머)
- 네이티브가 자주 쓰는 외래어. faux pas(실례), carpe diem(찬스를 잡아라, 지금을 즐겨라), prima donna(자기 중심적인 여성), aficionado(정열적인 애호가, 열렬한 팬), voila(자, 보시라), ciao!(그럼 안녕), hasta la vista(또 봐), buenos dias(안녕하세요, 낮 인사), noches(밤 인사)
- 분위기 있는 장소를 묘사할 때. quaint

7. 기분이나 생각을 제대로 전해주는 말들

- 기분을 강조할 때. couldn't be … / so …
- 찬성이나 반대할 때. I buy that. / I don't buy that.
- 마침 필요했어. It's just what the doctor ordered.
- 칭찬할 때
  - 성공 칭찬: good for you, awesome, great going!, I knew you could do it! this is incredible, way to go, well done, you did it.
  - 인격 칭찬: I admire you, there's nobody like you, you have a lot of patience, you're very creative
  - 업무 칭찬: brilliant idea, fantastic job, good job, good thinking, this is perfect, this is super.
  - 칭찬 겸한 격려: I appreciate your effort, looking good, keep up the good work, you tried hard, you tried your best.
- 칭찬에
  - 감사할 때: Thank you for the compliment. That means a lot coming from you. What a nice compliment!
  - 겸손할 때: That's not true. Not really. You're just joking. Don't say that.
  - 충고할 때(꿍꿍이 있는 칭찬에 대해): Stop brownnosing. 아첨은 관둬요.
Don't patronize me. 치켜 세우지마셈.
- 역할분담에 동의할 때. That's that.
- 이런 제발. Oh, please.
- 썰렁한 농담(lame joke)에 대꾸는. Give me a break. Oh, brother. Oh, no. Oh, jeez. Are we supposed to laugh? / Is that a joke?
- 무리한 요구를 받았을 때. Have a heart. Don't be so heartless. Don't you have a heart?
- 불만을 나타낼 때. Too bad. … suck!
- 나라면 그렇게 안해. I wouldn't.
- 곤란한 상황에서. Oh, god = boy. / good grief = god(이런 곤란하군)
- 귀찮게 됐다고 말할 때. pain in the neck / 어깨통증 stiff neck / 어깨주무르기 neck rub
- 어려운 말을 꺼낼 때. you see..
- 결론을 말할 때. the truth is… / to tell you the truth
- 의견을 강조, 확실히 해둔다구 할 때. make no mistake
- 진심으로 감사할 때. I owe you. / IOU note 차용증
- 결단을 촉구할 때. It's now or never. / Now is the time to act. / You have to act now. / There's no waiting.
- 정반대 두 상황 표현도 가능. some
- 비슷한 처지라구 위로 할 때. join the club

8. 친근감을 높여주는 말들

- 친구를 우연히 만나면. How's it going? / How goes it? / How are you? / How's the good word?
- 이야기 꺼낼 때.(well), you know(what?) / Guess what?/ listen.. / I'm telling you..
- 괜찮아요. No problem
- 좋아요, 식은 죽 먹기지. No problemo
- (부탁을 기꺼이 받아들일 때) 괜찮을 거 같아유. sounds good(fine)
- 가볍게 의견을 물을 때. How does that grab you? / How do you think it happened? / What do you think?
- 음식맛을 칭찬할 때. It's finger lickin' good(delicious).
- 내가 낼께. It's on me. / Let me get it. / Let me treat you. / I'll get it.
- 축약발음들(친근감 더하는). Forget about it. = fuhgeddaboudit / Would you give me that. = wajagimmetha / What did you do. = whaddayado / I don't know. = i dunno / i've got to do. = I gotta go. / It's going to rain. = it's gonna rain / Do you want to go. = yawannago
- 응원. break a leg! / hang in there / keep trying / don't give up / I know you can do it / I'm counting on you / have fun / do it / come on / go! go! / good luck!
- 운에 대한 표현들. good luck / out of luck / just my luck(운도 없지) / it was just luck(운이 좋았을 뿐입니다 - 겸손) what a stroke of luck! 저런
- 가볍게 위로할 때. I hate it when that happens.

9. 적절한 일상대화법

- 가벼운 제안에 답할 때. Sure. / Sounds good. / That would be nice.
- 정말로 고마울 때. I'd(really) appreciate that.
- 고맙다는 말에 댓구할 때. It's nothing. / No problem. / No worry. / It's easy. / No big deal. / It's all right. / My pleasure. / 농담 - I'll be sending my bill.
- 가벼운 거절. I'm fine. / Thanks. But no thanks.
- 동감이야. You got that right. / You're telling me. / You're right.
- 바로 그거야. Hit the nail on the head.
- 장담한다. You bet! / Wanna bet? / No problem.
- 정말? For sure? / Are you sure? / For real? / Really?
- 진심이야? Are you serious? / You're crazy. / You're kidding.
- 좋은 생각이군. Good thinking(idea). / I got it!(좋은 생각이 있어)
- (부탁하는 사람에게) 그런 걱정 허덜 말어. Say no more. No more. Okay. Sure
- 공감할 때. Say no more, okay. Sure.
- 놓친 말을 다시 물어볼 때. You said it. You can say that again. / You got that right 〉 that's right / That's the truth / What was that? / Come again? / Go where? / Said what?/ To where? / Excuse me? / I beg your pardon.
- 길을 모른다 할 때. sorry, I'm clueless. / I'm afraid i can't help.
- 술이나 음료를 따를 때. 괜찮습니다. Say when. ➔ That's enough(fine). - That's a little too much. - Could I have about half that much? - This much is okay?

- 이대로 괜찮아. I like it as it is.
- 행동을 재촉할 때. Let's get going. Let's hurry.
- 세상 참 좁아. It's a small world.
- 건강하세요. gesundheit(독일어에서), bless you(기침한 사람에게), good health

상황별 표현정리

(1) 회의, 모임

- **Please be seated.**
- **Please have a seat.** 자리에 앉아 주십시오.
- **Please welcome, Mr. John Smith.** 존 스미스 씨를 소개합니다.
- **We are happy to have you with us.** 모시게 되어 기쁘게 생각합니다.
- **Let's give him a big hand.** 이 분께 큰 박수를 부탁드립니다.
- **Whose turn is it?** 이번에 누구 차례지요?
- **You're on next.** 다음은 당신 차례입니다.
- **Please give us your opinion.** 의견을 말씀해 주세요.
- **May I have your attention for a while, please?** 잠시 제게 주목해 주십시오.
- **Let me take an example.** 제가 예를 하나 들어 보겠습니다.
- **Let's take a coffee break.** 잠깐 동안 쉬도록 합시다.
- **I agree with you.** 나도 당신과 같은 의견입니다.
- **I'm in favor of the plan.** 나는 그 계획에 찬성합니다.
- **Stick to the topic, please.** 주제와 부합되는 말만 해 주십시오.
- **The meeting is off limit.** 그 회의에는 출입금지입니다.
- **Let's call it a day.** 오늘은 이만 끝냅시다.
- **Let the meeting be called to order.** 개회를 선언합니다.
- **Pass them out, please.** 그걸 쭉 돌려 나눠 갖도록 하세요.(서류 따위)
- **Let's get to the point.** 본론으로 들어갑시다.
- **Don't change the subject.** 화제를 바꾸지 마세요.
- **Take a note.** 메모하세요.
- **Let me jot it down for you.** 메모해 드리죠.
- **Whose turn's next?** 다음은 누구 차례지요?
- **Let's speak in turn.** 순서대로 얘기합시다.
- **It's your turn.** 당신 차례입니다.
- **He cleared his throat.** 그 사람은 목청을 가다듬었다.
- **I'll get right to the point.** 바로 요점만 말씀드리겠습니다.
- **I am very happy to give you my opinion.** 내 의견을 알리게 되어 기뻐요.
- **As I recall, she would be Miss Kim.** 내 기억으로는 그 여자가 미스 김일 겁니다.

- **That's all I know about it**. 그것밖에 아는 것이 없습니다.
- **That's all I can think of at the moment**. 지금 생각나는 것은 그것밖에 없습니다.
- **What else do you want to know**? 또 뭐 알고 싶은 것 없습니까?
- **Does anyone have any questions so far**? 여기까지 다른 질문은 없습니까?
- **I was tongue-tied**. 나는 말이 안 나왔어요.
- **The cat got his tongue**. 그는 할 말을 잃었다.(긴장해서)
- **That reminds me**. 그러니까 생각나는군요.
- **I know it is a fact**. 그것이 사실이라는 것을 알고 있어요.
- **How did the idea strike you**? 어떻게 그런 생각을 해냈죠?
- **That makes sense to me**. 일리가 있는 말이군요.
- **Put yourself in my shoes**. 입장을 바꿔 놓고 생각해 보세요.
- **You're just talking out of the other side of your mouth**! 당신은 딴청을 부리고 있군요.
- **It is a little too optimistic to think so**. 그렇게 생각하는 것은 너무 안일해요.
- **Please hear me out**! 제 이야기를 끝까지 들어 주세요!
- **Are you with me**?
- **Do you follow me**? 제 말을 이해 하시겠어요?
- **You left out one word**. 당신은 한 마디를 빠뜨렸어요.
- **I will take back my words**. 제가 한 말 취소하겠어요.
- **He thought his visitor's attention was wandering**. 그는 상대방이 건성으로 듣고 있는 것 같다고 생각했어요.
- **We had very heated arguments over the issue**. 우리는 그 문제에 대해서 한바탕 입씨름을 벌였어요.
- **Let's discuss it over a beer**. 맥주 한 잔 하면서 토의합시다.
- **We quarreled over the case but soon made up**. 우리는 그일로 다투었으나 곧 화해했어요.
- **We had a man-to-man talk**. 우린 남자 대 남자로 이야길 했습니다.
- **I don't want to hasten to the conclusion**. 성급하게 결론을 내리고 싶지는 않아요.
- **I have this hang-up that is hard for me to overcome**. 저로선 해결하기 힘든 문제가 하나 있습니다.
- **Excuse me, that's out of the topic**. 미안합니다만 그 말은 주제를 벗어난 이야기입니다.
- **The truth struck home**. 진실은 정곡을 찔렀어요.
- **What's the problem here**? 여기는 대체 뭐가 문제라서 그런 거예요?
- **He lost face at the meeting**. 그는 모임에서 체면을 잃었어요.
- **She said something under her breath**. 그 여자는 뭔가를 작은 소리로 소곤거렸다.
- **Her cheeks went red as a rose with shame**. 그녀의 두 빰은 부끄러운 나머지 홍당무가 되었어요.
- **Let's get the meeting over by** 7. 일곱 까지는 회의를 끝냅시다.
- **Is there any set time for the morning break**? 아침 휴식시간이 정해져 있나요?
- **Let's take a break for ten minutes**. 10분간 쉽시다.
- **Let's take a ten-minute break**. 10분만 쉬도록 합시다.
- **It's getting near tea time**. 티 타임이 거의 되어 가네요.
- **Let up for a while and have some coffee**. 잠시 손을 놓고 커피를 드세요.

- **Are there any seconds?** 재청 있습니까?
- **I second the motion.** 재청합니다.
- **All those in favor of the motion sya aye.** 그 동의안에 찬성하는 분은 '예'라고 대답하시오.
- **All those against the motion say nay.** 동의안에 반대하는 분은 '아니오'라고 대답하시오.
- **We motion that the convention rule be amended.** 우리는 대회 규칙의 개정을 동의합니다.
- **The board of directors turned down the porposal.** 이 사회는 그 제안을 부결시켰다.
- **It's up in the air.** 아직 결정되지 않았습니다.
- **It was a unanimous decision.** 그것은 만장일치로 결정되었습니다.
- **Did you make up your mind?** 결정하셨습니까?
- **Which side are you on?** 당신은 어느 편입니까?
- **Are you for or against it?** 당신은 찬성입니까, 반대입니까?
- **I'm not against it.** 나는 그것을 반대하지 않습니다.
- **I feel the same way.** 나도 마찬가지 생각입니다.
- **I'm all for it.** 나는 전적으로 찬성합니다.
- **I whole-heartedly agree with you.** 나도 진심으로 동의합니다.
- **Whatever you do, I'm with you.** 당신이 무엇을 하든지 나는 당신 편입니다.
- **He is on the other side of the fence.** 그는 반대하고 있습니다.
- **This is off the record.** 이건 비공식입니다.
- **How did the meeting turn out?** 회의 결과는 어떻게 되었습니까?
- **How did the meeting go?** 모임은 어땠어요?
- **The meeting was a great success.** 회합은 대성공이었습니다.
- **The meeting was called off because of bad weather.** 일기가 나빠 그 회의는 취소되었습니다.
- **Unlike last year, most of the speeches this year were cut-and-dry.**
  지난 해와는 달리 금년의 연사들은 대부분 무미건조했습니다.
- **Who gave the opening address?** 누가 개회사를 했습니까?
- **Our plans are all up in the air.** 우리 계획은 아직 미정입니다.
- **We listed her among our society.** 그녀를 우리 모임의 회원으로 가입시켰습니다.
- **The members are from all walks of life.** 회원들은 각계각층의 사람들입니다.
- **Who has the last word in your circle?** 너희 서클에서의 결정권은 누가 쥐고 있니?
- **At first you'll feel out of place.** 처음에는 서먹서먹하게 느끼실 거예요.
- **I felt so out of place.** 분위기에 어울릴 수 없었어요.
- **He attended the meeting as if nothing had happened.** 그 사람은 아무 일 없었던 듯이 모임에 나갔다.
- **This chair just squeaks on its own.** 이 의자는 저절로 삐걱거리는군요.
- **How much is the membership fee?** 입회비는 얼마입니까?
- **The membership is open to all for free.** 누구든지 가입비 없이 회원이 될 수 있습니다.
- **Did Bill show up at the meeting?** 빌이 모임에 나타났어요?
- **No, he never showed up.** 아뇨, 그림자도 보이지 않았어요.

(2) 학교, 학업

• **Which college are you attending**? 어느 대학에 다니십니까?
• **I'm attending UCLA**. UCLA에 다니고 있습니다.
• **What are you majoring at**? 무얼 전공하십니까?
• **I'm majoring at Education**. 교육학을 전공하고 있습니다.
• **What grade are you in**? 몇 학년입니까?
• **What school did you go to**? 어느 학교를 나오셨습니까?
• **What class are you**? 몇 년도에 졸업했습니까? 몇 학번입니까?
• **How many courses are you taking this semester**? 이번 학기에는 몇 과목이나 수강신청을 했습니까?
• **I'm taking 19 credit**. 19학점을 수강하고 있어요.
• **I got a hundred on the English test**. 영어시험에서 100점을 받았습니다.
• **I better hit the books**. 공부를 해야겠어요.
• **I had a blind date today**. 나는 오늘 미팅했어요.
• **Many students are working at part time jobs**. 아르바이트하는 학생들이 많아요.
• **Where do you go to school**? 어느 학교에 다니십니까?
• **I'm a graduate of Harvard University**. 저는 하버드 대학 졸업생입니다.
• **He's ahead of me in school**. 그는 제 학교 선배입니다.
• **Bayside High School is my Alma Mater**. 베이사이드 고등학교가 제 모교입니다.
• **She's fresh out of high school**. 그녀는 고등학교를 갓 나왔습니다.
• **I've got six months to go until the graduation**. 6개월만 있으면 졸업하게 돼요.
• **He is a college drop out**. 그는 대학 중퇴자입니다.
• **I shared the boarding room with him in my school days**. 학창 시절에 나는 그 사람과 하숙방을 같이 썼어요.
• **She was kicked out of the university**. 그녀는 대학에서 퇴학당했다.
• **He worked his way through college**. 그는 고학으로 대학을 나왔어요.
• **She won the first place in a debate**. 그녀는 논평에서 1등상을 탔어요.
• **Did you sign up for a computer class**? 컴퓨터 강좌에 신청하셨어요?(이름만 적어 넣는 신청)
• **Do you have a part time job**? 아르바이트를 하고 있나요?
• **I don't want to cut class**. 나는 결강하고 싶지 않습니다.
• **He's busy preparing for class**. 그는 수업준비하느라 바쁩니다.
• **You will never get the answer**. 네 머리로는 아마 답을 못 구할걸?
• **How much are three and five**? 3 더하기 5는 얼마입니까?
• **How much is Thirty minus twenty-five**? 30 빼기 25는 얼마입니까?
• **How much is three times five**? 3 곱하기 5는 얼마입니까?
• **How much is twenty divided by four**? 20 나누기 4는 얼마입니까?
• **Oh, I know the answer to that problem**. 아, 그 문제에 대한 답을 알겠어요.
• **Have you ever studied Portuguese**? 포르투갈 어를 공부하신 적이 있나요?

- **He's still hung up on the bad grades he got last semester.**
  그는 아직도 지난 학기에 받은 좋지 않은 성적에 집착하고 있어요.
- **He rated the work a '10'.** 그는 그 작품에 만점을 주었습니다.
- **What's the book about?** 그게 무슨 책이죠?
- **I'm working for my degree.** 학위를 얻으려고 공부하는 중입니다.
- **I don't think I have a mathematic brain.** 저는 수학적인 머리가 없는 것 같아요.
- **I applied for a scholarship.** 나는 장학금을 신청했다.(서류 등을 구비한 신청)
- **I got scored high enough to attend Yale University.** 나는 예일대학에 입학할 만큼 높은 점수를 얻었어요.
- **This has been a hard course for me.** 이건 제게 어려운 학과였어요.
- **We had to learn it by heart.** 우리는 그것을 암기하지 않으면 안 되었어요.
- **I've been studying all day, and I'm sick and tired of it.** 종일 공부를 했더니 넌더리가 나는군요.
- **Examination are at hand.** 시험이 코앞에 닥쳤어요.
- **I think I have to hit the books now.** 이제 공부를 좀 해야 할 것 같아요.
- **He seems to be getting on very well at school.** 그는 학교 성적이 매우 좋아진 것 같아요.
- **I'm bent on the outcome of the experiment.** 난 그 실험결과에 큰 기대를 걸고 있어요.
- **Speaking of school, how are your grades this term?** 학교 얘기가 났으니 말인데, 이번 학기의 학점은 어때요?
- **He passed the whole grades by cheating.** 그는 전 학년을 컨닝을 해서 다녔다.
- **I'm pleased to announce that everybody got good results.**
  모두가 좋은 성적을 얻었다고 발표하게 되어 기쁘군요.
- **His lectures are interesting but he never seems to come to the point.**
  그의 강의는 재미있지만 결코 목적이 없는 것 같아요.
- **She is at the top of her class.** 그녀는 반에서 1등이예요.
- **She is a cut above her classmates.** 그녀는 동급생 중에서도 두드러집니다.
- **Looks like I'm far behind my classmates.** 내가 우리 반에서 제일 뒤떨어진 것 같아요.
- **He's a bear for physics.** 그는 물리학에 뛰어난 사람이예요.
- **Who'd you get for biology?** 생물 선생은 누구로 했니?
- **Everyone has passed the exam with flying colors.** 누구나 시험을 잘 보았어요.
- **If you don't study hard, you'll not be able to make the grade in English.**
  열심히 공부하지 않으면 영어에서 합격점을 따기 어려울걸요.
- **What if we're late for the class?** 만일 수업에 늦으면 어떻게 하지요?
- **I've run out of ink.** 잉크가 다 떨어졌어요.
- **His foolish question exasperated the teacher.** 그의 바보 같은 질문이 선생의 신경을 몹시 건드린 거예요.
- **What does the board say?** 게시판에 뭐라고 씌어 있는 거예요?
- **She is giving me piano lessons in exchange for her English classes.**
  그녀는 내가 영어를 가르쳐 주는 댓가로 나에게 피아노를 가르쳐 줘요.
- **I took him for a teacher.** 나는 그가 선생인 줄 알았어요.
- **I like to sit way in the back.** 나는 맨 뒷자리에 앉기를 좋아해요.

- **A hen party at six tonight at the students' hall.**(cf.: stag party)
  학생회관에서 오늘 저녁 6시에 여학생 파티가 있습니다.(참고: 남학생만의 파티)
- **The story is all about a tutor's love affairs.** 그 이야기는 온통 가정교사의 연애사건에 관한 것이었어요.
- **I'm copying my friend's English tapes.** 친구의 영어 테이프를 복사하고 있어요.
- **You always stick together.** 너희들은 항상 붙어다니는 구나.
- **She's an easy-going teacher.** 그녀는 천하태평의 선생이예요.
- **The course I took was above me.** 내가 들은 과목은 나한테 너무 어려웠어요.
- **As far as I am concerned, he is a professor.** 내가 아는 바로는 그분은 교수예요.
- **Now is the round-up time.** 또 학교에 가야 되는구나.(방학이 끝날 때 가기 싫다는 뜻)
- **There's nothing wrong with hard work.** 열심히 공부하는 게 나쁠 건 하나도 없어요.
- **Why are you being kept in after work?** 너희들은 왜 방과 후에도 잡혀 있니?
- **You will be in a fix if the teacher catches you.** 선생님한테 잡히면 곤란해해질 걸.
- **What are you going to be when you grow up?** 넌 커서 뭐가 될 거니?
- **We went on a chartered bus.** 우리는 전세 버스로 갔습니다.
- **I groped for my glasses.** 나는 안경을 찾으려고 더듬거렸어요.
- **He is burning the midnight oil.** 그는 밤중까지 공부를 해요.
- **How did the test turn out?** 시험결과는 어떻게 되었나요?
- **She's really up on Korean history.** 그녀는 한국사에 정통합니다.
- **I hope I'll go down in history as a famous English professor.**
  나는 역사에 유명한 영어 교수로 기록되기를 희망합니다.

(3) 칭찬

- **The way you dress shows very good taste.** 옷을 입으신 것을 보니 취미가 고상하시군요.
- **It's very nice of you to say so.** 그렇게 말씀해 주시니 고맙습니다.
- **You did a fine job.** 참 잘하셨어요.
- **That's beautiful!**(wonderful, great) 멋있군요.(굉장하군요, 놀랍군요)
- **You're so nice!** 친절하기도 하셔라!
- **That's very nice of you.** 친절도 하시네요.
- **That's the way.** 그렇지요, 그렇게 해야지요.
- **I am very proud of you.** 나는 당신이 자랑스럽습니다.
- **I didn't expect you to do such a good job.** 그렇게 훌륭하게 해내리라고는 미처 생각 못했어요.
- **For a beginner, you're pretty good.** 초보로서는 상당히 잘 하는군요.
- **You are the right man for the job.** 당신은 이 일에 안성맞춤입니다.
- **She is quite good with her hands.** 그녀는 손재주가 좋아요.
- **You've got a point.** 맞는 말입니다.(잘 지적하셨어요)
- **You look like a million bucks.** 참 멋지군요.
- **You look young for your age.** 나이에 비해 젊어 보이시는군요.

- **You have a very good memory**. 기억력이 참 좋으시군요.
- **What a cute baby**! 아이가 참 귀엽군요!
- **You have beautiful eyes**. 당신은 눈이 참 예쁘군요.
- **Oh, that's keen**! 어마, 멋있군요!
- **He's a gentleman in every sense of the word**. 그는 어느 모로 보나 신사입니다.
- **Joanne is very photogenic**. 조앤은 사진을 아주 잘 받아요.
- **You came out beautiful in this picture**. 이 사진에 아주 잘 나왔네요.
- **This picture flatters her**. 사진은 그녀의 실물보다 더 잘 나왔군요.
- **You're lovelier than your pictures**. 사진보다 실물이 더 예쁘네요.
- **You are well-built**. 신체가 좋습니다.
- **You look fit**. 건강해 보이시는 군요.
- **What's responsible for your good health**? 건강의 비결은 무엇입니까?
- **How do you keep fit**? 어떻게 그렇게 건강하십니까?
- **How do you keep in shape**? 어쩜 그렇게 날씬하세요?
- **I stick to my diet and exercise a lot**. 다이어트를 계속하고 운동을 많이 해요.
- **You look prosperous**. 요즘 경기가 좋은 모양이군요.
- **You're all dressed up**. 자네 쪽 뺐군.(굉장하게 차려입었군.)
- **You look nice in your new shirt**. 새 셔츠를 입으니 보기가 좋군요.
- **That tie goes well with your suit**. 그 타이는 당신 옷에 잘 어울립니다.
- **You look stunning in it**. 그거 참 잘 어울립니다.
- **It really looks good on you**. 그것은 정말 당신한테 잘 어울립니다.
- **You must be very popular**. 인기가 대단하시겠어요.
- **Where did you get such a nice tan**? 어디서 그렇게 멋지게(햇빛에 피부를) 태우셨어요?
- **I fell in love with you**. 나는 당신에게 반했습니다.
- **You flatter me immensely**. 과찬이십니다. 원 별 말씀을!
- **What a lovely couple you make**! 어울리는 한 쌍이군요!
- **You must be a man of ability**. 당신은 능력이 대단하시군요.
- **How come you speak such good English**? 어떻게 그렇게 영어를 잘하십니까?
- **You speak English without an accent**. 마치 미국 사람처럼 영어를 잘 하십니다.
- **You are in good command of English**. 영어를 훌륭하게 구사하시는군요.
- **She is cut out to be a nurse**. 그녀는 간호원으로는 적격이예요.
- **You got a good point**. 잘 지적해 주셨어요.
- **You've got it**! 맞아요, 바로 그거예요!
- **You made a tough decision**. 어려운 결심을 하셨군요.
- **You're an early bird, aren't you**? 당신은 참 부지런하시군요.
- **That's right. You have a very good memory**. 맞아요. 기억력이 썩 좋으시군요.
- **He is up on mathematics**. 그는 수학에 능해요.

- **You have an eye for fashion**. 패션에 대한 안목이 있으시군요.
- **He's a real egghead**. 그는 정말 머리가 좋아요.
- **He's such a bright boy**. 그는 머리가 참 좋은 아이예요.
- **He has a good head on his shoulders**. 그는 현명한(똑똑한) 사람이예요.
- **You always know the right thing to say**. 당신은 참 인사성이 밝으시군요.
- **She has a memory like an elephant**. 그녀는 기억력이 굉장히 좋아요.
- **She is quick-witted**. 그는 재치가 있어요.
- **You've got what it takes**. 그녀는 소질이 있어요.
- **You must be a walking encyclopedia**. 당신은 모르는 게 없군요.
- **You get a gold star for that**. 정말 잘했어요.
- **He is very handy with tools**. 그는 도구를 다루는 손재주가 있어요.
- **Is there anything you can't do**? 못하는 게 없으시군요.
- **I wish I were in your shoes**. 당신의 입장이 부럽습니다.
- **I wish I had your will power**. 당신 같은 강한 의지력 좀 있었으면 해요.
- **I admire you for sticking to your plans**. 계획에 충실하는 당신이 존경스럽습니다.
- **Look how well he's swimming**. 정말 그는 수영을 잘 하네요.
- **I owe my success to my father**. 저의 성공은 아버지 덕분이죠.
- **You are a cut above me**. 네가 나보다는 한 수 위야.
- **Do you weave**?(화병받침 따윌를) 당신이 짜셨어요?
- **I envy you for your ability to cope with the situation**. 그런 상황을 극복하시는 당신의 역량이 부럽습니다.
- **You are coming along well**. 아주 잘 하고 있어요.
- **She has it all over Ms. Sylvia in her ability to handle the machine**(**sittuation**).
  그녀는 실비아보다 기계(상황)을 다루는 데 있어 탁월합니다.
- **You got a brand-new bike**. 아주 새 자전거를 가지셨군요.
- **That's a good buy**. 그거 잘 사셨군요.
- **It's so very nice**. 그거 정말 좋은데요.
- **Where did you get all this nice furniture**? 이렇게 훌륭한 가구를 어디서 구했나요?
- **I had it specially made to order**. 그것을 특별히 맞추었습니다.
- **No wonder it is so nice**. 그래서 그렇게 훌륭하군요.
- **It's a real beauty**! 정말 근사한데요!
- **You have a lovely home**. 멋진 집을 갖이셨군요.
- **What a gorgeous fire place**! 벽난로가 굉장하군요.!
- **What a lay-out**! 모든 게 이상적으로 되어 있군요!
- **That's more like it**! 그게 더 근사하네요!

(4) 감사

- **You're doing me a big favor, Kim**. 김, 제가 큰 은혜를 입었습니다.

- **Thank you**. 감사합니다.
- **You're welcome**. 천만에요. Don't mention it.
- **Not at all**. 원 별말씀을요.
- **The same to you**. 당신도요.
- **You're more than welcome**. 천만에요(강조)
- **It's very nice of you to say so**. 그렇게 말씀해 주시니 고맙습니다.
- **It's very kind of you to help me with my English**. 제 영어 공부를 도와 주셔서 고맙습니다.
- **Thank you for everything**. 그저 감사할 따름입니다.
- **Thank you anyway**. 어쨌든 감사합니다.
- **Thank you very much indeed**. 정말 감사합니다.
- **I appreciate it very much**. 그점 정말 고맙게 생각합니다.
- **I would appreciate it**. 그렇게 해 주시면 감사하겠습니다.
- **Thank you for the ride**. 태워다 주셔서 감사합니다.
- **Thank you for giving me a lift**. 태워다 주셔서 감사합니다.
- **It was my pleasure**. 제가 오히려 고맙죠.
- **It's kind of you to say that**. 그렇게 말해 주시니 고맙습니다.
- **I'm all right now. Thank you**. 이젠 괜찮습니다. 고맙습니다.
- **Thank you, I'd like that**. 고맙습니다. 그거 좋지요.
- **I don't know how to thank you enough**. 어떻게 감사를 드려야 할지 모르겠군요.
- **How can I ever thank you?** 어떻게 감사를 드려야 할지 모르겠어요.
- **I can never thank you enough**. 얼마나 감사한지 모르겠어요.
- **Thank you very much for a nice evening**. 저녁시간 덕분에 재미있었습니다.
- **No thanks. I'd better not**. 감사합니다만, 사양하겠습니다.
- **Thank you very much, but I guess I'd better do it myself**. 감사합니다만, 제 스스로 해야 할 것 같습니다.
- **Thank you for your hospitality**. 환대에 감사드립니다.
- **I appreciate your consideration**. 여러모로 고려해 주셔서 정말 고맙게 생각합니다.
- **You've been a great help**. 큰 도움이 되었어요.
- **Thanks a million, Mr. Kim, for what you have done for me**.
  나를 위해 그렇게 해준 것, 정말 고맙게 생각하고 있어요, 미스터 김.
- **I hope I can repay you for it**. 보답해 드릴 수 있었으면 좋겠어요.
- **I'm only too glad to be able to help you**. 당신을 도울 수 있다는 것은 너무나 기쁜 일이죠.
- **Thanks just the same**. 저도 마찬가지로 감사합니다.
- **We've got to thank him for it**. 우린 그 일로 그 사람한테 감사를 해야 합니다.
- **The pleasure is all mine**. 천만의 말씀입니다.
- **Thanks. I'll pay you back in one month**. 고마와. 한 달 뒤에 갚을께.(돈을 빌릴 때)
- **How kind of you to say so**. 그렇게 말씀해 주시니 감사합니다.
- **I enjoy your company**. 동반해 주셔서 즐겁습니다.

- **I very much appreciate your hospitality and friendship.** 당신의 호의와 우정에 정말 깊은 감사를 드립니다.
- **I certainly enjoyed the evening.** 저녁시간 정말 즐거웠습니다.
- **I had wonderful time being with you.** 당신 덕분에 오늘 정말 재미있게 보냈습니다.
- **That was a wonderful dinner.** 훌륭한 저녁 식사였어요.
- **I'v enjoyed every moment we've had together.** 같이 보낸 모든 순간이 정말 재미있었습니다.
- **I appreciate you taking your time with us.** 저희와 함께 시간을 보내 주셔서 감사합니다.
- **Everything was delicious.** 모든 게 맛 있었습니다.
- **I'm glad you enjoyed it.** 맛 있게 드셨다니 고맙게 생각합니다.
- **Couldn't be better.** 더할 나위없이 좋았습니다.
- **You're a lifesaver.** 당신은 생명의 은인입니다.

(5) 여행

- **May I see your boarding pass, please?** 탑승권을 좀 보여 주시겠습니까?
- **What can I do with this bag, Mr?** 이 가방을 어떻게 할까요?
- **Please put it under your seat or in the overhead bin.** 의자 밑이나 머리 위에 있는 통 속에 놓아 두십시오.
- **How many more hours until we land in New York?** 몇 시간 더 가면 뉴욕에 착륙합니까?
- **How much farther is it?** 얼마나 더 가야 돼죠?
- **What time do we land in Chicago?** 몇 시에 시카고에 착륙할까요?
- **Are you going to serve dinner on this flight?** 비행 중에 저녁식사가 나옵니까?
- **What's the purpose of your visit?** 방문 목적은 무엇입니까?
- **What is your destination in the United States?** 미국에서 당신의 목적지는 어디입니까?
- **When do you plan to return to your home country?** 고국에 언제 돌아가실 계획입니까?
- **How long are you going to stay in this country?** 이 나라에 얼마동안 머물 예정이십니까?
- **How long has your daughter lived in the United States?** 댁의 딸은 미국에 얼마나 오래 살았습니까?
- **Take me to the Sharraton Hotel in Mahattan.** 맨하탄의 쉐라톤 호텔까지 부탁합니다.
- **How far is it from here?** 여기서 거리가 얼마나 되지요?
- **It'll take maybe thirty minutes this time of night.** 밤 이맘때면 아마 30분쯤 걸릴 겁니다.
- **About how much will the fare be?** 요금은 얼마나 될까요?
- **How long will it take?** 시간은 얼마나 걸릴까요?
- **I have to catch a plane. Can't you hurry?** 비행기를 타야 하는데요. 급히 갈 수 없을까요?
- **I'm going as fast as I can.** 최선을 다해서 가고 있습니다.
- **Do you have a single room available?** 1인용 방이 있습니까?
- **When are you checking in?** 언제 들어오시죠?
- **For how many nights, sir?** 며칠 밤을 주무실 겁니까, 손님?
- **I'd like to stay 3 nights and check out Saturday morning.** 3일 밤을 지내고 토요일 오전에 나가려고요.
- **I'd like a room, please.** 방 하나 있습니까?
- **Single or double, sir?** 1인용을 말씀하십니까, 아니면 2인용을 말씀하십니까?

- **The porter will take your bags.** 짐꾼이 가방을 운반해 드릴 겁니다.
- **Are you checking in now?** 지금 들어오시겠습니까?
- **What is the check-out time?** 방을 나가야 하는 시간이 언제입니까?
- **I'll be checking out tomorrow morning at eight.** 내일 아침 8시에 나가게 될 겁니다.
- **My room is too close to the elevator. Can I change it?**
  내 방이 엘리베이터에 너무 가까이 있는 데 바꿀 수 있을까요?
- **Sorry, sir. We're full.**
- **I'm sorry we're all booked up.**
- **I'm sorry, but we have no vacancy.** 죄송합니다. 방이 만원입니다.
- **Sorry, sir. Nothing else is vacant.** 미안합니다, 손님. 그거말고는 빈방이 하나도 없어요.
- **Can you give me a wake-up call at six?** 6시에 내 방으로 전화를 해서 좀 깨워 주시겠어요?
- **Hang on. I'll transfer your call to the front desk.**
  잠시만 기다리세요. 프론트 데스크로 전화를 돌려드리겠습니다.
- **Could you suggest some interesting places to visit?** 관광할 만한 데를 몇군 데 소개해 주시겠습니까?
- **Can you break a twenty dallar bill?** 20불짜리 뿐인데 잔돈으로 거슬러 주시겠어요?
- **Sure, if you don't mind getting a lot of singles.** 물론이죠. 1불짜리 여러 개로 드려도 괜찮으시다면.
- **I can break it for you.** 제가 거슬러 들릴 수 있습니다.
- **You have to pay in advance.** 미리 지불하셔야 합니다.
- **I'd better call and reserve the tickets in advance.** 전화를 해서 표를 미리 예약해야 겠습니다.
- **We have about five more hours to go.** 5시간쯤 더 가면 돼요.
- **Fill her(it) up. Unleaded, please. Unleaded**로 한 탱크 가득 채워 주세요.
- **Do you want me to check your oil and water?** 기름과 물도 점검해 드릴까요?
- **Self-service is a few cents cheaper per gallon than Full-service.**
  셀프서비스는 풀서비스보다 갤런당 몇 센트가 싸요.
- **Is this pump self-service?** 여기는 본인이 직접 기름을 넣는 곳인가요?
- **Do you want your car washed?** 세차를 원하세요?
- **I hear you're(returning) going to L.A.** L.A.에(돌아)가신다면서요.
- **When are you leaving?** 언제 떠나십니까?
- **Are you going to stay there permanently?** 가셔서 영주하실 계획인가요?
- **How are you going?** 어떻게 여행하실 건가요?
- **Are you flying?** 비행기로 가시나요?
- **Where are you headed?** 어디 가십니까?
- **I'm on my way to New York.** 뉴욕에 가는 중입니다.
- **I have four weeks off for vacation.** 4주간 휴가입니다.
- **What's your destination?** 목적지가 어디신가요?
- **Which street am I on now?** 지금 여기가 몇 가입니까?
- **How do I get to the post office from here?** 여기서 우체국을 어떻게 갑니까?
- **It's three blocks north on Clark Street.** 클락 스트리스에서 북쪽으로 세 블럭에 있습니다.

- **Which way do I go to get to Clark Street.** 클락 스트리트를 가려면 어느쪽으로 가야 합니까?
- **You are on Clark Street.** 지금 여기가 클락 스트리트입니다.
- **How far is the Museum from here?** 여기서 박물관까지는 얼마나 멉니까?
- **It's about two blocks from here.** 여기서 약2블럭 정도입니다.
- **Where are from?** 고향이 어디세요?
- **Seoul is famous for its Seoul Tower.** 서울은 서울타워로 유명합니다.
- **The traffic was bumper to bumper this morning.** 오늘 아침에 교통이 굉장히 복잡했어요.
- **How long does it normally take?** 보통 때는 시간이 얼마나 걸리나?
- **I left my house at the usual time and it took two hours to get here.** 보통 때와 같은 시각에 집을 떠났는데 여기까지 2시간이나 걸렸어요.
- **How often do you have flights to New York?** 얼마나 자주 뉴욕행 비행기가 있습니까?

(6) 식당

- **I'd like a cheese burger and a small coke, please.** 치즈 버거와 콜라 작은 것으로 주세요.
- **Will that be all?** 그게 전부인가요?
- **Yes, that's all.** 네, 그게 다예요.
- **Here or to go?** 여기서 드실건가요, 아니면 가지고 가실건가요?
- **To go.** 가지고 갈 겁니다.
- **Two large french fries to go.** 프랜치 프라이 큰 것을 가지고 갈 겁니다.
- **Do you know of any good(French) restaurants?** 좋은 식당을 알고 계십니까?
- **There's one on Main Street. They serve excellent French food.** 메인 스트리트에 한 곳 있습니다. 그곳의 불란서 음식맛이 아주 좋습니다.
- **How did you enjoy your dinner last night?** 간밤의 저녁식사가 어땠어요?
- **It was terrible.** 형편없었습니다.
- **It was very good.** 아주 좋았어요.
- **The food was cold, the service was bad and the meals were overpriced.** 음식도 차고, 써비스는 엉망이고, 값은 터무니없었거든요.
- **Excuse me. Is this seat taken(occupied)?** 실례합니다. 이곳에 누가 앉으세요?
- **Do you have any particular restaurant in mind?** 특별히 마음에 드는 식당이라도 있으세요?
- **Have you ever tried(tasted) fried shrimp?** 새우튀김을 먹어 본(맛보신) 적이 있나요?
- **Do you like Korean food?** 한국 음식을 좋아하세요?
- **What's your favorite Korean food?** 가장 좋아하는 한국 음식은 뭔가요?
- **What kind of Korean food would you like to(have?)try?** 무슨 종류의 한국 음식을 드시겠어요?
- **I really don't know. Why don't you order for me?** 전 정말 모르겠어요. 제 대신 주문해 주세요.
- **O.K. How about trying bulgogi? It's like roast beef.** 좋아요. 불고기를 드시는 게 어때요? 로스트 비프같은 거예요.
- **Fine. Whatever you say.** 좋아요. 당신이 주문하는 대로 할께요.
- **Are you ready to order now, sir?** 주문하시겠습니까, 손님?

- **Yes. I'll have tomato soup, roast beef and mashed potatoes.**
  네. 토마토 수프, 로스트 비프, 그리고 메쉬 포테이토를 주세요.
- **What do you recommend**? 무얼 먹었으면 좋겠어요?
- **What's the special of the day**? 오늘 특별요리가 뭐죠?
- **How do you want the steak**? 스테이크는 어떻게 해드릴까요.
- **Well-done(Rare, medium), please.** 바짝 구워(덜 익혀, 중간쯤 익혀) 주세요.
- **Anything to drink**? 마실 것은 어떻게 하시겠어요?
- **Glass of water will be fine.** 물이면 되겠어요.
- **And you, sir**? 그리고 손님은?
- **Same here.**
- **I'll have the something.** 나도 같은 것으로 하겠습니다.
- **I'll have what she's having.** 저 여자분이 하시는 걸로 하겠습니다.
- **How often do you eat out**? 얼마나 자주 외식을 하십니까?
- **Lunch is on me.** 점심은 내가 사죠.
- **Let's go dutch.** 각자 부담합시다.
- **Drinks are on me.** 마실 것은 내가 내죠.
- **What was the name of the food we ate on our last visit**? 전에 왔을 때 뭘 먹었었죠?
- **Don't eat too much bread. Save room for the main course.**
  빵만 너무 먹지 마세요. 정식이 들어갈 자리는 비워두셔야죠.
- **Would you care for a cup of coffee**? 커피 한 잔 드시겠습니까?
- **Do you take sugar or cream in your coffee**? 커피에 설탕이나 크림을 넣으세요?
- **I like mine plain.** 저는 플레인으로 하죠.
- **I like mine black with pinch of sugar.** 저는 설탕을 조금만 넣어서 블랙으로 하죠.
- **May I have a refill.** 한 잔 더 주시겠어요.(refillable일 경우)
- **Miss, may I have the check**? 아가씨, 계산서 좀 가져 오세요.
- **You're holding up the line.** 당신 때문에 줄이 이동이 안 됩니다.
- **I couldn't(can't) help it.** 어쩔 수가 없(었)어요.
- **This milk(meat) has gon bad.** 이 우유(고기)가 상했어요.
- **This bread's stale.** 이 빵이 오래되어 딱딱해요.
- **This beer is stale.** 이 맥주가 김이 빠졌군요.
- **These eggs are rotten.** 달걀이 상했군요.
- **This cream is sour** 이 크림이 상했군요.

(7) Konglish 정리

핸드폰 hand phone → cellular phone // → 자동차핸들 handle → steering wheels/wheels // 리모콘 remocon → remote control // 츄리닝 training → sweat suit // 모닝콜 morning call → wake-up call // arbeit → part-time job // 아이쇼핑 eye shopping → window shopping // 호치키스 hotchikiss → stapler // 백미러 back mirror → rear-view mirror // 오토바이 autobi(ke) → motorcycle/motorbike/bike // 백넘버(등번호) back number → number/uniform number/jersey number // 싸인(서명) sign → signature / autograph BB → beeper/pager // 골인 goal in → goal / make a goal // 포볼(야구) four ball → base on balls // 명함 → business card / name card // 파이팅(응원) fighting → go/come on/cheer up // 비닐하우스 vinylhouse → greenhouse // 선글라스 sunglass → sunglasses // 에어컨 aircon → air-conditioner/air/AC // 애프터서비스 A/S(after service) → warrantee service // 원샷(한번에 마시기) one shot → bottoms up / slam it // 가격할인 D.C → discount // 비닐봉투 vinyl bag → plastic bag // 탤런트 talent → actor/actress // 써클, 동아리 circle → club/student group // 와이샤쓰 Y-shirt → dress shirt/white shirt/shirt //(남녀의) 미팅 meeting → blind date // 롤러 브레이드 roller blade(상표명) → inline skate // 몸에 맞는 볼(야구) dead ball → hit by pitch ball // 스탠드 등 stand → desk lamp // 콘도 condo → timeshare/resort hotel // 드라이버 driver → screw driver // 폴라 셔츠 polar → shirt turtleneck // 썬탠 크림 suntan cream → sunscreen lotion / sun block cream // 카셋트(녹음기) cassette → cassette player // 샤프(연필) sharp pencil → mechanical pencil // 컨닝(부정행위) cunning → cheating // 공책, 노트 note → notebook // 아파트 apart → apartment // 황금시간대 golden time → prime time // 에로영화 ero movie → soft porn / NC-17 movie

* **미국의 영화관 개봉영화의 상영등급은 모든 연령층의 관람이 가능한 G에서 17세 미만은 관람이 불가한 NC-17까지 총 5등급으로 분류되어 있다.**

- G - General Audiences(All Ages Admitted) - 모든 관객(모든 연령층 적합)
- PG - Parental Guidance Suggested 부모 동반(부분적 아동 관람 부적합)
- PG-13 - Parents Strongly Cautioned 부모 주의(부분적 13세 미만 부적합)
- R - Restricted 제한(17세 미만은 부모나 성인 보호자 동반 요망)
- NC-17 - No Children under 17 admitted(17세 미만 관람 가)

* **성인영화 adult movie[film], X-rated movie[film], 도색 영화(桃色映畵) a sex film, pornography, blue movies(속어)**

// 투피스 two-piece(여성용 수영복) → suit / business suit // 슈퍼 / 슈퍼마켓 super → supermarket // 빌라 villa(대저택, 호화별장) → duplex/house // 애인 lover(섹스파트너) → dear/darling/sweetheart/honey * CC? =college sweetheart // 포켓볼(당구) pocketball → pool // 휘발유 oil → gas / gasoline // 사이다 cider(사과주스) → 7-Up / Sprite // 공중전화 박스 telephone box → phone booth/telephone booth // 팬티 panties(여성용) → underwear(남녀의 속옷 모두를 통칭) 등산 mountain climbing(등반) → hiking // 파마 perma → perm/permanent // 오디오/전축 audio → stereo/audio system // 아마(선수) ama → amateur //(자동차의) 악셀 accel → accelerator(영)/gas pedal(미) // 매스컴 mass com → mass media/mass communication // 볼펜 ball pen → ball-point pen/pen //(눈에 끼는) 렌즈 lens → contact lenses/contacts // 헬스(헬스클럽) health → health club /gym/fitness center // SF 영화(공상과학영화) SF movie → sci-fi(발음[saifai])/science fiction // 프림(커피에 타는) prim → cream // 프로(%) pro → percent // CF(방송광고) CF → commercial/TV ad. // A/S 센터 A/S center → repair shop/the shop // 콘센트 consent → outlet /socket // 깁스 gibs → cast // 맥가이버 칼 Macgyver knife → Swiss Army knife // 펑크 난 타이어 punk tire → flat tire // 메이커(유명상표) maker → famous-maker/brand-name // 리어카 rearcar → pushcart // 스킨십(피부접촉) skinship → touchy-feely // 본드(접착제) bond → glue // 워커(신발) walker → hiking boots // 바바리(코트) Burberry(상표명) → trench coat //(자동차)썬팅 sunting → window tinting // 무스탕 mustang → leather jacket // 자동차 경적(클랙슨) klaxon(상표명) → horn // 잠바 jumper → jacket // 영화의 특수효과 F.X. → special effects //

*** 컴퓨터 자판 영어**

- \# Crosshatch(두 줄 평행선을 십자로 그리다), number sign, hash(전화기의 우물정자), pound
- * Asterisk
- $ Dollar Sign
- % Percent Sign
- ! Exclamation Point
- @ At Sign
- & Ampersand
- ^ Circumflex

*** fare, fee, toll, dues, rate, price, charge 각종 요금**

- fare는 목적지까지 가는 데 드는 요금을 뜻합니다. fare는 동사로 '가다'입니다. 작별인사 'farewell'은 말 그대로 '잘 well 가 fare'가 되는 거죠. 잘 가라는 인사로 Fare you well! 이라고도 합니다.
- Toll은 교통수단의 통행료입니다. Toll gate에서 내는 고속도로 통행료나 항만 이용료가 그 예입니다. 자릿세, 텃세에도 쓰이고 사고의 댓가인 사상자 수를 나타내기도 합니다. 통화료로도 쓰입니다.
- Fee는 무형의 전문직 서비스나 각종 수수료입니다.(Tuition fees 수업료, an admission fee 입장료, a patent fee 특허료, an insurance fee 보험료, a fee for consultation 변호사 등의 상담료) 등과 같이 씁니다.
- Due(duty 의무 관련 어휘)에 s가 붙은 Dues는 응당 지불해야 할 회비로, 일정기간마다 내는 경우에 씁니다. A Membership fee는 입회비인 반면 membership dues는 월회비가 되구요.
- Rate는 비율 ratio과 관련이 있는 요금으로 시간이나 하루 단위로 계산하는 경우에 쓰입니다. 렌터카, 도서나 DVD 대여, 숙박비 등이 그 예가 되겠습니다. Rent도 rate처럼 대여하는 요금인데 집이나 기계, 설비와 같이 규모가 좀더 크고 그에 따라 월이나 년 단위로 기간이 긴 경우에 쓰입니다.
- Price는 'precious 가치있는'와 비슷하게 생겼죠? 대개 물건의 가치, 값을 나타냅니다.
- Charge는 서비스나 노동의 대가, 일하는 노력에 따른 요금을 나타냅니다.

(8) 영어 은어

가십걸 끝날 때마다 나오는 xoxo는 love라는 뜻을 가진 말이 있고, because를 줄여 쓴 cuz가 있고, 흑인을 비하해서 말하는 nigga라는 단어 있었는데, 이 단어는 흑인 앞에서 절대 쓰면 안 된다고 들었어요. 그리고 영화에서 많이 나오는 damn, goddamn, shit은 우리나라 말의 '제길'보다 좀 수위가 높은 말이구요. 그리고 돈이라는 말로는 dollar 대신에 buck이라는 단어를 훨씬 많이 쓰구요.

1. **left-handed**(부정한, 가짜의)
2. **Junk call**(녹음된 목소리로 상품 홍보 판매하는 전화)
3. **natural**(천부적 재능의 소유자, 천재)
4. **late-nighter**(철야족)
5. **dry out**(금주하다)
6. **man-day**(1인 1일의 작업량)
7. **inside job**(내부에서 생긴 범죄)

8. **eye-grabber**(강하게 남의 눈길을 끄는 것)
9. **flophouse**(값싼 여인숙)
10. **eighty-six**(주방장이나 웨이터가 손님에게 서비스를 거부하다)
11. **multitongued**(일관성이 결여된)
12. **hit list**(삭감계획안)
13. **gallows bird**(극악무도한 흉범)
14. **give the go-by**(무시하다)
15. **hard sell**(강매)
16. **hard-hat**(건설노무자, 노동자)
17. **exes**(비용, 경비)
18. **shotgun wedding**(상대 처녀의 임신으로 마지못해 하는 결혼)
19. **diff**(차이)
20. **ass-wipe**(화장지)
21. **safe**(피임기구)
22. **sack**(해고, 면직)
23. **rot**(헛소리)
24. **pushover**(매우 간단한 일, 식은 죽 먹기)
25. **nosy**(참견하기 좋아하는)
26. **shy**(시도)
27. **dig up**(우연히 옛날 것을 발견하다)
28. **killout**(굉장히 멋진 것)
30. **bone-weary**(몹시 지친)

[질문]: '양다리 걸치다'란 다란 의미의 다른 영어 표현은?

[답변]: He is a two timer 라는 two timer 외에도… Sit on both sides of the fence. Play double. Play(have) it both ways. 같은 것들이 있다

[질문]: **Monkey Around**의 의미는?

[답변]: 이 표현은 학생이 하라는 공부는 안 하고 빈둥빈둥 놀기만 할 때 혹은 누구에게 뭔가 물었는데 대답은 안 하고 쓸 데 없는 소리만 할 때 등등 일처리가 느리고 시간을 허비할 때 쓰이는 표현이며, 또한 깊은 관계까지 맺을 정도로 누구와 교제한다는 의미도 갖고 있답니다. 이와 유사한 의미를 지닌 표현으로 mess around란 표현이 있습니다.

You are not paid to sit and monkey around. You are paid to do a job.
(앉아서 놀기만 하라고 당신에게 급료를 주는 것이 아니고 일을 하라고 주는 겁니다.)

Occasionally I feel like doing nothing but monkeying around.
(때때로 난 일을 안 하고 놀고만 싶어질 때가 있어요.)

저자소개

최용선 / 현) 김포대학 관광영어과 교수
- 건국대학교 영어영문학과(문학사)
- 건국대학교 대학원 영어영문학과(문학석사)
- 건국대학교 대학원 영어영문학과 영어학 전공(문학박사)
- 아리랑 TV, EBS 교육방송 감수
- 한국전문대학협의회 학과평가 및 기준개발위원
- 영상영어교육학회, 한국대학영어교육학회 이사
- 교육인적자원부 장관 표창(유학생 유치 정책 실적)
- 논문 : 영어학습자들을 위한 영어의 성차별에 대한 연구 외 다수
- 저서 : Basic English for College Students, Basic English Conversation
  호텔관광실무영어, TOEIC 등 다수

왕영균 / 현) 동남보건대학교 항공관광영어과 교수
- 한국대학영어교육학회 부회장
- 논문 : 관광사이트 번역 시 발생하는 문화적 차이에 대한 연구,
  아버지 그림자 극복하기
- 저서 : College English, TOEFL & TOEIC PREP

인지
생략

| 호텔관광실무영어 |

발 행 일 2014년 2월 5일 초판 인쇄
2014년 2월 25일 초판 발행
저 자 최용선, 왕영균
발 행 인 김시동
발 행 처 정문각
서울특별시 마포구 백범로 104, 봉화빌딩 4층
출판등록 1990년 10월 25일 9-246호
전 화 02)713-0421~3
팩 스 02)704-6265
전자우편 jungmunk@unitel.co.kr
홈페이지 www.jungmunkag.co.kr

정 가 **18,000원**

ISBN 978-89-7742-541-5 93740